THE
ORGANIC
GOURMET
FEAST OF FIELDS

THE ORGANIC GOURMET
FEAST OF FIELDS

WRITTEN AND COMPILED BY TRACY KETT

Robert
ROSE

THE ORGANIC GOURMET

For complete cataloguing data, see page 6.

DESIGN AND PAGE COMPOSITION:	MATTHEWS COMMUNICATIONS DESIGN INC.
ILLUSTRATIONS:	SHARON MATTHEWS
PHOTOGRAPHY:	MARK T. SHAPIRO
ART DIRECTION/FOOD PHOTOGRAPHY:	SHARON MATTHEWS
FOOD STYLIST:	KATE BUSH
PROP STYLIST:	CHARLENE ERRICSON
MANAGING EDITOR:	PETER MATTHEWS
INDEXER:	BARBARA SCHON
COLOR SCANS & FILM:	POINTONE GRAPHICS

Cover photo: Bouquet of Greens Wrapped in Smoked Salmon on a Crisp Potato Pancake (page 92)
Back cover photo: Grilled Pizza with Caramelized Corn Salsa and Sweetened Greens (page 126)

Distributed in the U.S. by:
Firefly Books (U.S.) Inc.
P.O. Box 1338
Ellicott Station
Buffalo, NY   14205

Order Lines
Tel: (416) 499-8412
Fax: (416) 499-8313

Distributed in Canada by:
Stoddart Publishing Co. Ltd.
34 Lesmill Road
North York, Ontario
M3B 2T6

Order Lines
Tel: (416) 213-1919
Fax: (416) 213-1917

Published by: Robert Rose Inc. • 156 Duncan Mill Road, Suite 12
Toronto, Ontario, Canada M3B 2N2   Tel: (416) 449-3535

Printed in Canada
1234567 BP 01 00 99 98

CONTENTS

Canadian Cataloguing in Publication Data

Kett, Tracy

    The organic gourmet : feast of fields

Includes index.

ISBN 1-896503-83-7

1. Cookery (Natural foods).   2. Cookery, Canadian.   I. Title.

TX741.K47 1998   641.5'637   C98-931594-0

ACKNOWLEDGEMENTS

Many people helped me put together this cookbook in the two short months I had to research, write and compile it. First, thanks go to Lorene Sauro who initiated this cookbook project to celebrate the 10th anniversary of Feast of Fields. From finding a publisher and acting as the Knives & Forks liaison to testing most of the dessert recipes, providing information on organic baking ingredients and reviewing the manuscript, Lorene has kept her enthusiasm and commitment to the project without fail.

The Organic Gourmet wouldn't be a cookbook without the co-operation and participation of the talented chefs across Canada who have continued to support Knives & Forks and organic agriculture. This includes *all* of the people who have participated in Feast of Fields since 1989. The majority of the recipes in this cookbook have been served at past Feast of Fields in Southern Ontario or Vancouver. Other chefs and restaurateurs – some of whom had never heard of Knives & Forks until my telephone call – have graciously contributed their recipes to support the use of seasonal, local ingredients and a sustainable food system. Thank you to every chef and restaurateur who helped make *The Organic Gourmet* representative of what's cooking all across the country.

As well, thanks go to the recipe testers who made sure that the recipes worked in a home kitchen. While they tried to keep to the original recipes as much as possible, they also modified them to yield successful results and attributed measures, directions and times when necessary. To David Cousins, Carolyne Hoshooley, David Moore, Lisa Rollo, Gillian Talacko and Christine Thomas, thank you.

Thanks also go to: Don Blakney, who reviewed the section on organic food and agriculture; Andrea Robertson and Adrienne O'Callaghan, who co-ordinated the Vancouver chefs and their recipes; Lauren Boyington, who wrote some of the biographies; Tomás Nimmo, who supplied some of the sources; the Knives & Forks board members who supported this project; and the members who helped narrow down the recipes from the hundreds that have been served during the past nine years. (This was no easy feat.) Other people, such as the organic growers I interviewed and the people who put me in touch with valuable contacts, are too numerous to list but I do appreciate every bit of information that has been passed my way.

And finally, thanks to Brad Cundiff, who reviewed the front sections and who's been working and living amid cookbooks and chaos for two months – well, for 13 years.

Tracy Kett
Toronto, 1998

INTRODUCTION

The 10th anniversary of Feast of Fields – Knives & Forks' signature event – is the inspiration for *The Organic Gourmet*. What originally began in 1989 as a modest walkabout featuring urban cuisine in a rural setting has become an event that guests and participants eagerly anticipate year after year. Imagine strolling through a sweet-smelling field sampling dozens of the freshest, most succulent organic creations – accompanied by organic and local wines and beers – and you will get a taste of Feast of Fields.

This successful fund-raising initiative was created by Knives & Forks, Advocates for Organic Agriculture. The group, founded in 1989 by chefs Jamie Kennedy and Michael Stadtländer, is a non-profit coalition of southern Ontario organic producers, environmentally concerned chefs and other food professionals and enlightened consumers who are committed to raising the understanding and support for organic agriculture and environmental responsibility.

While the event is intended to be a leisurely, sumptuous experience, the underlying theme of Feast of Fields is the connection between those who grow our food and those who eat it, and the interdependency of all living things.

To emphasize the plant-to-plate connection, chefs are often partnered with organic farmers as early as the spring so that both supply and demand are confirmed. At the event, organic growers are invited to sell their delicious selections of organic products and answer questions about their operations and philosophies. As well, nonprofit groups provide additional information about organic agriculture, the environment, fair trade and other related issues. Knowledge is power, and the sense of community is strengthened and energized through this kind of dialogue.

And energy abounds at Feast of Fields. Generous, enthusiastic and talented people make this event popular: From the chefs who create amazing dishes over a simple campfire or gas barbecue and the wineries and breweries that continue to innovate with their products, to the dedicated, hardworking organic farmers who work year round to grow the food we eat and the hundreds of volunteers who are committed to the organic movement.

Of course, there is mouth-watering fare to ensure the event's success. It's no coincidence that Feast of Fields takes place in September, the pinnacle of harvest season. This gives chefs an opportunity to take advantage of the unlimited harvest bounty at their doorsteps and what they deliver is incomparable.

This does mean, however, that some of the recipes in this cookbook share similar ingredients because they were in season: corn, red peppers, apples, tomatoes, beets, squash, potatoes and plums are familiar items on the menu. Regional cooking is also prevalent at Feast of Fields so wild mushrooms, wild rice, goat cheese, smoked fish and maple syrup often make appearances too. Chefs tend to work with what they have – organically and locally – and you should too.

If you're flipping through this cookbook in the spring, adapt one of the recipes to the season and try a vinaigrette drizzled over freshly picked asparagus or fiddleheads. Or if a recipe with corn in it sounds appealing in the winter, by all means, buy that organic corn in your store's freezer section. *The Organic Gourmet* should be used any time of the year to bring together new ideas and flavors to your home. It's not a cookbook to be slavishly followed; improvise, skip a few steps, substitute ingredients and have fun.

You may notice that some of these recipes have another thing in common – the way the dish is presented. One of the unique features of Feast of Fields is that the food is created to be eaten by hand, which eliminates unnecessary paper plates and other disposable items. Chefs have ingeniously served their fare wrapped in crêpes and lettuce leaves, nestled in vegetable cups and tomatoes, layered on top of croquettes and cornbread and even offered on cedar planks and pieces of slate.

This marriage of food and nature is not just a southern Ontario event – Feast of Fields has been spreading across Canada. FarmFolk/CityFolk, a Vancouver-based coalition of urban and rural people who are committed to the development and maintenance of a just and sustainable food system, has hosted its own Feast of Fields for the past several years. FarmFolk/CityFolk organizes other events and initiates a variety of projects and networks with organizations related to food, environment, health and agriculture.

In the Ottawa area, a group of chefs and farmers has organized one Feast of Fields to date, while Earth to Table in Calgary has taken the concept and turned it into a dinner. Groups in Halifax, Montreal and Winnipeg have expressed interest in hosting the event as well. (For more information on FarmFolk/CityFolk and Earth to Table, see "Organic Sources," pages 21-24.)

Funds raised through Knives & Forks' Feast of Fields help support organic agriculture and the promotion and understanding of growing, cooking and eating organics. This includes developing projects such as *The Organic Gourmet* and an educational video for school groups. Some of these funds are also donated to other organizations and projects that share similar philosophies including the Canadian Organic Growers, the Organic Crop Improvement Association, Seeds of Diversity Canada, the Guelph Organic Conference and a cable-television program on organic agriculture.

The front section of this cookbook explains the importance of organic agriculture and some specifics about organic food. By no means is it an in-depth discussion of the issue but it is a good introduction. For more information about organic agriculture, contact a local organization such as a chapter of the Canadian Organic Growers. The organic sources listed on pages 21-24 will give you a few groups to start with.

What follows these introductory sections is the heart of the cookbook – the recipes. Most of the ingredients in the recipes can be found organically in large cities across North America. And indeed, Knives & Forks encourages you to use as much organic fare as possible. Unfortunately, availability of organic food in smaller or more remote centers varies depending on the community, so use organic ingredients if possible and encourage your retailers to carry more.

All of the recipes in *The Organic Gourmet* have been tested and some have been adapted to work better in a small-scale kitchen at home. We have, however, tried to change as little of the recipes as possible to preserve the integrity of the chef's original. But feel free to spice the dishes according to your own taste, embellish on an idea, simplify a recipe (yes, you can buy smoked fish or roasted red peppers instead of doing it yourself!), mix and match the different recipe components and substitute or skip ingredients where you see fit.

With *The Organic Gourmet,* you can recreate some of the delicious innovations served at past Feast of Fields. To complete the experience, transport yourself to a place beside a rippling stream or among grape-laden vines or surrounded by maple forests. Enjoy!

Organics
FOOD AS IT WAS MEANT TO BE

Have you ever pulled a carrot fresh from the garden and eaten it, dirt and all? Or picked a tomato straight off the vine and bit into it, juice dripping down your chin? Bliss. Organic produce has the ability to retain that heavenly fresh-from-the-earth flavor. What you are tasting is the actual fruit or vegetable, pure and simple. There are no pesticides, fungicides or waxes to mask or contaminate the flavor.

Contrary to what many people think, organic food is not simply "granola" food composed of veggie burgers, yogurt and alfalfa sprouts, and eating organic food does not necessarily mean eating a vegetarian diet. Today, almost any fresh, frozen or processed food has an organic counterpart.

Just walk into any one of the growing number of stores selling organic food and you might be surprised at what you can find alongside the standard fare: fresh heirloom fruits and vegetables, interesting grains and legumes, Muscovy duck – even frozen prepared organic dinners such as vegetarian pizzas and chicken pot pies. The range of organic offerings is enormous.

And it's getting even bigger. Sales of organic food in North America have been increasing 20 to 30 percent annually over the past decade, and organic food is now the fastest-growing segment of the natural-foods market. According to a February 1998 *Time* magazine article, sales of organic food totalled US$4 billion in the United States – more than 22 times the 1981 total of US$178 million. And the future looks bright: The U.S. Department of Agriculture predicts that within 10 years organic produce will make up 10 percent of all of the produce sold in the United States.

Superior flavor is what counts

Many people believe that organic food is inferior in quality to conventional food. In fact, the reverse is true. Many chefs use organic ingredients in their kitchens because such foods are *superior* – in terms of appearance, flavor, freshness and shelf life.

Sure, some organic fruits and vegetables may appear blemished and imperfectly shaped. But that's because they are not sprayed or treated with chemicals to create perfect-looking produce. And imperfections *do* exist in commercial produce – they just never reach the stores. Truckloads of commercial apples, for example, are rejected for size, shape and imperfections when they are sorted at the orchard. In organic orchards, because smaller volumes are produced and there is less emphasis on cosmetics, there is less waste. Besides, the superior flavor outshines any visual oddity.

Another belief about organic food is that it's much more expensive than conventionally farmed food. But this is not always the case – particularly in the peak of growing season, when organic produce is comparable in price (sometimes cheaper, in fact) than commercial produce. Of course, there are some organically grown and processed foods that cost more; but there are many reasons for this. The primary one is that the "real" cost of commercial food is higher than what consumers actually pay at the supermarket.

Organic food defined

Quite simply, organic food is produced without the use of synthetic or artificial fertilizers, pesticides, herbicides, fungicides, fumigants, growth regulators, antibiotics, preservatives, dyes, additives, chemical coatings or irradiation.

In the case of processed foods, most organic-certification standards allow for a small percentage of non-organic ingredients. However, with a can of certified-organic chili, for example, you can be assured that it is made exclusively from ingredients (beans, tomatoes, onions, chilies, etc.) grown without toxic chemicals, and that it was processed without additives such as xanthan gum, disodium guanylate or maltodextrin. And if the organic chili contains beef, you'll know that the cow was raised without using hormones, growth enhancers or antibiotics, that it was fed organic grains throughout its life, and that it was butchered according to organic-certification regulations.

The benefits of organic agriculture

What organically farmed soil has that conventional soil doesn't is an abundance of life: Millions of insects, bacteria and other micro-organisms are busy nourishing, recycling, replenishing, aerating and enriching the soil.

In order to protect our lands, food productivity and ecological diversity, organic farmers take a holistic and harmonious approach to their business. In other words, they try to manage their crops, land and livestock as nature intended – with respect. Organic growers work with nature, rather than trying to dominate it. By following organic practices such as companion planting, crop rotation, cultivating by hand, weeding, composting and mulching, organic growers maintain healthy, fertile soil that will continue to produce successful harvests year after year.

Diversity is a very important ecological component of organic farming. In organic agriculture, crops are continuously rotated to maintain sustainable soil with balanced nutrient levels. This results in reduced pest and disease problems. Monoculture farming (the same crop planted every year in the same soil) on the other hand, drastically strips away precious topsoil and depletes the soil of its health, leaving it less resistant to infestations and diseases.

On organic farms, pest problems that do arise can be controlled by organic or natural remedies and techniques such as using biodegradable botanical soaps and sprays, setting pheromone traps (traps that use an insect's natural secretions as a lure), releasing predator insects to eat the crop-ravishing ones and picking unwanted insects off by hand. Planting a secondary crop to attract insects that are beneficial to the primary crop or to divert insects that are attracted to the primary crop is also practised in organic agriculture.

While modern conventional farming uses large quantities of petroleum resources, organic farming tends to use less petrochemical energy and more renewable resources. One example can by found on Martha and Ken Laing's 100-acre (40-hectare) certified-organic Orchard-Hill Farm near St. Thomas, Ontario. The family uses organically reared draft horses to plow and cultivate their fields and cut and rake their hay. A horse-drawn ridge-till planter allows them to plant corn, soybeans and spelt without tilling, thereby saving the soil from erosion and saving the Laings labor. The horses also help fertilize the farm, producing a rich soil with good root structure for their crops.

Organic agriculture also seeks to minimize agriculture's contribution to the planet's environmental problems such as acid rain, global warming, loss of biodiversity and desertification. Healthy topsoil, for example, contains large quantities of carbonaceous material so it lowers greenhouse CO_2 gas levels and holds more water, which reduces both flooding and drought.

You get what you pay for

A common complaint from consumers is that organic food is expensive. What many people don't realize is that the real cost of conventional food is much higher than what we pay at the check-out counter. Our tax dollars already go toward government subsidies for university and government chemical-research projects, export subsidies and direct support to large-scale commodity farmers. Canadian taxes also pay for medical care and environmental clean-up costs that may result from the use of toxic chemicals. Add a dramatic loss of topsoil caused by conventional agriculture and that conventional bunch of carrots may be costing our society much more than an organic one.

At the height of harvest season, local organic produce is often sold for the same price as conventional produce. At other times, that cost can be twice the price, depending on the source and time of year.

Here are a few points to consider when evaluating the price of organic agriculture:

• Most farms are small family-run operations that are not highly profit-driven and seldom receive government subsidies or support for organic research projects.

• Organic food generally takes longer to grow than conventional food as chemical growth hormones and fertilizers can speed up the rate of growth of conventional crops by about 10 percent.

- Produce is usually picked when it is ripe – unlike conventional food, which, to allow for transportation time, is picked unripe and before it is fully developed. Consumers can savor organic food at its peak flavor and nutritional value because it is usually sold soon after it is harvested. Once again, this means the organic farmer has invested more time in the crop than a conventional farmer.

- The majority of organic distribution is done on a small scale, so the transportation costs are often higher. Organic farmers usually grow small amounts of several things which are harvested at different times, unlike conventional farms that have large quantities of one commodity and a distribution network firmly established.

- Losses during distribution can be higher than for conventional produce due to the lack of fumigants and wax coatings added for shipping.

- Organic-certification bodies charge their members for annual inspections and the use of their certification labels, which verify that the food has been truly grown and processed organically.

- There is a minimum three-year transition period (the time it takes chemically treated soil to gradually wean itself off "drugs") for farmers who want to apply for certification; during this period farmers usually do not receive a full income.

As demand for organic food increases, studies indicate that prices will eventually decrease. That's simple economics. In the meantime, it's worth considering what the price of organic food is worth to you.

A plateful of pesticides

Besides the fact that organic food can taste better than conventional produce and meat – because organic varieties are often chosen based on flavor rather than yield and cosmetics – food that is grown organically is healthier for consumers, the environment and the livelihood of farmers.

As food and water expert David Steinman reports in his book *Diet for a Poisoned Planet: How to Choose Safe Foods for You and Your Family* (1990, Harmony Books), 183 pesticide residues have been found in conventionally grown peanuts and 110 in raisins. Rating these foods as the most pesticide-saturated foods, Steinman advises eating only organic peanuts and raisins if possible.

Other foods that are heavily sprayed with chemicals are tomatoes, citrus fruits, apples, lettuces and beans. Unfortunately, washing or peeling produce will not eliminate most of the toxic residues because the pesticides often spread throughout the entire vegetable or fruit.

Residual toxins can have a cumulative effect on the health of consumers. Take a conventionally raised cow for example. In addition to the growth enhancers and antibiotics the cow is occasionally given, the cow, is also given commercially grown feed. This feed has been sprayed and treated with a number of chemicals, which are then ingested by the cow and become concentrated within its body. Consumers, in turn, eat the cow along with a multiple dosage of toxins.

According to Pollution Probe's *Additive Alert! What Have They Done to Our Food?* (1994, McClelland & Stewart Inc.), toxic chemicals often concentrate in animal fat. For this reason, the Toronto-based environmental organization recommends that consumers watch their intake of animal products, remove the skin and trim off the fat from poultry, fish and meat and eat low-fat dairy products. Consumers eating organic food, on the other hand, do not have to concern themselves with taking such precautions and can indulge worry-free.

Several studies have found that the possible short- and long-term human health effects of agricultural chemicals are numerous and range from respiratory problems in field workers (despite hazardous working conditions, farmers and their employees often work without any kind of safety clothing or respiratory protection) to severe allergic and asthmatic reactions, reproductive disorders, cancer and degenerative diseases in both consumers and farm workers.

One of the most alarming aspects of the use of chemicals in conventional farming is that most of them serve no real purpose. According to research done at Cornell University, 500 million kilograms

(1.1 billion pounds) of pesticide chemicals are applied in North America every year. Of that amount, 99.9 percent miss the target organism.

Another astonishing fact about pesticides comes from John Bede Harrison, author of *Growing Food Organically* (1993, Waterwheel Press): "In 1945, only 13 kinds of pests were found to be resistant to the pesticides then available. Forty-five years later, over 500 types of pests had developed resistance. Today there are over 50,000 commercial products manufactured to combat resistant pests."

How do all these toxic chemicals affect our planet? To start with, they can deplete the earth of its nutrients and its diversity of life forms, pollute our land, water and air – which in turn harms the wildlife that depends on them – and lead to considerable soil erosion. Singularly, these concerns are serious, together they are disastrous.

Is it really organic?

Certification bodies have been established around the world to assure consumers that the food they are buying is indeed organic. Unfortunately, because there are many certification bodies worldwide, there is not just one symbol to look for; certification logos come in all shapes, sizes and colors.

At the moment however, these logos and their certification bodies are the *only* way consumers can ascertain whether the food is truly organic. Federal regulations and standards on labeling organic food in the United States and Canada are still works-in-progress – as is an international standard being drafted by the United Nations.

After the U.S. Department of Agriculture (USDA) released its proposed organic standards in December 1997 it was immediately besieged with an outpouring of concern and objections from farmers, chefs and consumers from around the world. This outrage was driven by the fact that the USDA completely ignored the advice of the National Organic Standards Board – the very board that the USDA created to recommend acceptable organic guidelines – and suggested allowing food that has been irradiated, genetically engineered or "fertilized" with sewage sludge to be classified "organic."

In May 1998, U.S. Agriculture Secretary Dan Glickman announced that in response to the approximately 200,000 comments received by the USDA, fundamental revisions would be made to the initial guidelines. A revised proposal will be released later in the year, he promised, for more public comment.

North of the border, a Canadian standard for organic agriculture is in its fifth draft explains Canadian Organic Advisory Board (COAB) president and certified-organic farmer Gordon Hamblin. If approved by the 42 organic-certification bodies in Canada and then the Standards Council of Canada, a national standard for Canadian organic food could be in place by the end of 1998.

What a national organic standard would mean is that members of all of the Canadian certifying bodies would use the same guidelines and organic certification logo, thereby eliminating any confusion for consumers buying Canadian organic products. This new logo would officially designate that the item displaying it met Canada's official standards for organic food, which Hamblin believes will help protect and promote the organic industry at home and abroad.

Until national standards are established, consumers must keep their eyes open for several different logos. One of the most familiar certification logos belongs to the Organic Crop Improvement Association (OCIA). OCIA is a farmer-owned and -controlled group and the most established international certification body, with approximately 30,000 certified members worldwide.

Other certifying bodies in Canada include the Society of Bio-Dynamic Farming and Gardening (known as Demeter), the Organic Crop Producers and Processors, Quality Assurance International, Fédération de l'Agriculture Biologique du Québec, Canadian Organic Certification Co-operative, Island Organic Producers Association, Peace River Organic Producers Association, Organic Producers Association of Manitoba, Maritime Certified Organic Growers and Nova Scotia Organic Growers Association.

Among the many certifying bodies in the United States are Oregon Tilth, Organic Verification Organization of North America, the Organic Growers and Buyers Association, Farm Verified Organic, Inc., United States Assurance Laboratories, Scientific Certification Services, California Certified Organic Farmers, Hawaii Bio-Organic Growers Association, Organic Growers of Michigan, New Mexico Organic Commodity Commission and Virginia Association of Biological Farming.

While there are many different certification bodies, most of the organizations operate in a similar manner. They require that their comprehensive production and processing standards be met and that farmers re-apply each year for certification. (Before a farm is even allowed to apply, it must be managed organically for at least three years, the period that is deemed necessary to "detoxify" the land.) An independent third-party inspection of the farm is also conducted annually, with professional inspectors examining everything from the farm's history and its future prognosis to crop information and field management.

Another field-to-table assurance for consumers is that certified farmers must maintain a continuous paper trail so that their products can always be traced back to them. These records can also verify that the feed the farmers have been giving their livestock is indeed certified organic or that the botanical soaps used on the farms adhere to organic regulations.

Naturally, to operate a certification body takes money, money that comes from farmers who are often already financially burdened. To become certified, farmers must pay hundreds of dollars for applications and inspections plus a royalty on any food they sell that bears the certification body's logo or name.

Of course, these certification costs are passed on to the consumer but as Toronto pastry chef and Knives & Forks past-president Lorene Sauro notes, clear audit trails are important to consumers – individuals and food professionals alike. Through her bakery businesses, Beyond Words Desserts and Nature's Song Organic Bakery, Sauro has introduced organic ingredients to the general public by creating thousands of decadent organic desserts for grocery stores and restaurants across Canada. " 'Certified organic' is the only guarantee consumers have. I'd rather pay a little more and know that I'm getting truly organic food than pay less and be lied to," she notes.

Some farmers are seeing the importance of certification for both consumers and themselves. Hamblin reports that currently there are more than 1,800 certified-organic growers in Canada, almost triple the number around in 1989.

So look for certification logos or certifier names on your groceries to confirm that you are buying veritable organic products.

Where to buy organic food
More and more stores are carrying organic food to meet the increasing demand from consumers, says Debra Boyle, founder and president of Pro Organics Marketing Inc., a Vancouver-based company that began distributing organic food in Canada in 1989. Of the consumers eating organically, Boyle estimates that 55 percent eat only organic food.

Boyle has seen a tremendous increase in sales not only in her business but all across North America. As a director of the Organic Trade Association, Boyle says that in recent years she has seen sales growth of 30 percent annually.

One company to reap the rewards of this escalating business is Whole Foods Market based in Austin, Texas, the largest chain of natural- and organic-food stores in North America. Started in 1980, the company became publicly traded in 1992 and now has more than 75 stores across the United States. The only other national natural- and organic-food chain is Wild Oats Market, Inc. based in Boulder, Colorado, which also has three stores in Vancouver, B.C.

A company the size of Whole Foods Market naturally has its own distribution network (seven warehouse centers across the United States); however most stores carrying a wide variety of organic stock don't have such a system in place.

For its 1,000 regular customers across Canada, Pro Organics provides services such as sourcing, warehousing, transportation and distribution of organics directly from 500 certified-organic farms. When its Toronto warehouse opened in November 1996, Boyle reports that large grocery chains such as Loblaws, Pusateri's, Longo Brothers and Fortino's made a firm commitment to carry organic food and began doubling their organic stock.

A good distribution network is essential for smaller businesses too, says Jennifer Grant, owner of Harmony Whole Foods in Orangeville, Ontario and also a board member of the Organic Trade Association and of the Canadian Health Food Association. Since Pro Organics moved into Central and Eastern Canada, "I've been ordering more and selling more," Grant notes. And Pro Organics has been delivering, "quality and quantity and it's certified."

Grant also supports locally grown "transitional" produce because she feels that the farmers need encouragement to become certified. (There is some concern among organic advocates about how long a farm should be able to retain its "transitional" status before applying for certification.) "We live in the richest farmland in the world and I'm selling carrots from California," Grant says. With Grant and other retailers taking the same stand, perhaps more growers will see the real market potential and will "wake up and smell the organic coffee," she adds.

As well as buying organic food in stores, consumers can also support organic farms by shopping at local farmers' markets or through programs such as Field to Table's Good Food Box Program in Toronto, which offers its participants a box of certified-organic produce twice a month every month. Similarly, community shared agriculture (CSA) programs are also a good way to support local organic farmers and are becoming more popular and prevalent across North America.

Generally, the CSA program works like this: In the spring consumers buy a "share" of a CSA farm, which helps the farmer purchase seeds, tools, labor, etc. for the growing season and ensures that s/he has consumers for the farm's products and receives a fair and steady income.

What the investor gets in return is a weekly box of fresh organic produce from about June to October. Similar to other investments, there is some risk. For instance, if there is a pest problem that can't be solved organically, there may be fewer tomatoes, or if there's no rain, there might not be any lettuce for a month. Depending on the farm, some shareholders are also welcome to work on the farm, which often brings a new understanding and respect for organic farmers and food production.

Free-range vs. organic chickens and eggs

Are free-range and organic chicken and eggs the same? No. While organic chickens are free range, free-range chickens are not necessarily organic. "Free range" means that the chickens are free to go outside of the barn where they can enjoy the sunshine, fresh air and nutrients gleaned from scratching in soil. (It should not mean simply free to roam outside of cages in the barn, which is how some stores and farms interpret the term.)

The differences between organic and free-range chickens are what the chickens eat, how much space they have, how they're raised and also how they are processed. Organic chickens are fed organic grains, mineral vitamins and other organic mixtures to keep them healthy and tasty and generally are free to flap their unclipped wings in and out of their cageless barns and are air-chilled when processed to preserve their natural flavor.

Still, true free-range chickens are better than conventionally raised chickens. Certified-organic egg farmer Gerald Poechman of Poechman Family Farm in Walkerton, Ontario believes that free-range birds and eggs are a good first step for consumers. "Consumers have no context or background information about organic farming and 'free range' is culturally more acceptable [than conventional farming]. However, egg producers have to start to recognize the consumers' desire for organic eggs," he says.

Since they began selling certified-organic eggs in 1994, Gerald and Marlene Poechman have not been able to keep up with market demand. With 1,800 dozen eggs produced a week – making the farm one of the largest commercial organic-egg producers in Canada – Poechman says that they are "100 percent oversold."

Similarly, there is a tremendous market for certified-organic chickens says Carol Fennema in Ancaster, Ontario. She and her husband John run Fenwood Farm, which processes 3,000 chickens every 10 weeks. Both the Fenwood and Poechman farms sell to stores in Ontario and Quebec and while they believe that many customers buy their products for environmental and health reasons, both cite taste as a principal factor as well.

Besides special blends of organic feed that supplement the nutritional and taste value of the chickens and eggs, the flavor of both products are enhanced by other measures. "Our chickens are air-chilled for several reasons," Fennema explains. "First, air-chilling guarantees that our certified-organic chickens are not mixed up with other birds in the large water baths [used in conventional processing], which is very important to our customers. Second, in a cold-water bath, birds can gain about 10 to 20 percent water and our customers are paying for chickens, not water. And third, air-chilling preserves the chicken's natural juices and is far tastier."

On the egg side, the Poechmans developed a unique nesting-box system: "There's a plastic screen underneath the nests that's sloped so the eggs always roll away from the bird," Poechman explains. "This way they cool more quickly and remain fresher." The eggs from the farm's 3,600 layers are collected by the Poechman children every night.

Unlike conventional egg farms that often have cages stacked eight high, the two buildings at the Poechman Family Farm allow each bird two square feet (.18 square meters). In reality "each has the run of the pen," he says. The Poechmans also have about 100 roosters to create a more social environment, he adds, which helps the chickens feel more secure and content.

Poechman feels that organic farming is gaining more credibility and that small farmers are starting to understand that an organic business is feasible. In the next year he predicts that he'll be able to contract other organic egg producers to help fill his market demand.

The pure satisfaction of organic meat

Many people associate organic food with vegetarianism. But in organic agriculture, plants rely on animals and vice versa, and the two have a strong symbiotic relationship. Consumers are also usually more comfortable with organic husbandry than conventional farming because the animals are treated more humanely throughout their lives.

But what is organic meat? Organic meat comes from an animal that has not been fed anything grown with toxic or synthetic fertilizers, pesticides, herbicides, fungicides or fumigants; has not been given any kind of growth hormone, antibiotic or genetically engineered product; has been conceived by organically raised animals; and has been butchered and processed following organic regulations.

Organically raised animals are also given more space and freedom than conventionally raised animals. For example, Harro and Anke Wehrmann of Huron Game Farm in Ripley, Ontario allow each of their 350 certified-organic wild boars 1 acre (0.4 hectare) on which to wander and graze. "They need their space and they have a tremendous social structure and a certain travel pattern," explains Harro Wehrmann. "We have 650 acres [260 hectares] so we let them roam and the rest of the land is used for growing hay and grains, which we rotate from field to field so they always have fresh pasture.

"We believe in all aspects of organic farming," Wehrmann continues. "We have to respect all animals and handle them in a stress-free manner." Because organic livestock are reared in such a humane manner and organic farmers maintain impeccable pasture-management practices, the animals are generally in good health. With organic farming, prevention of maladies is emphasized over treatment of them. When a disease or infection does strike an animal, it is nursed back to health without the use of chemical treatments, although it is given a little tender loving care.

Organic farmers give a lot more personal attention to their animals than conventional farmers, says Don Blakney, who with his partner John Camilleri operates Poplar Lane Organic Farm in Alliston, Ontario, where they raise sheep and grow certified-organic produce. "You mingle with your livestock and they become as familiar as your kids," he explains. "You can sense immediately when something's amiss. You've got to determine a problem early on because organic applications may not be as effective later on in the disease."

Blakney points out that according to a University of Guelph study, this personal attention – not growth hormones – also leads to quicker weight gain. "Animals that are secure, comfortable, have good bedding and are fed properly tend to gain weight faster," he reports.

Good feed may make a difference to the animal's weight, but, more importantly, it also makes a difference to its taste. "Feed makes the meat," Wehrmann says concisely. Similar to any craft, raising livestock is an art form and requires talent. Particularly for game animals, which aren't marbled, meat is the taste carrier Wehrmann adds. His wild boars are real gourmets, he notes, and eat everything from his special mix of organic grains, acorns and berries to wild plants and Jerusalem artichokes.

One of the final stages an organic livestock farmer must oversee is the butchering process. All meat in Canada, organic and non-organic, is butchered according to federal and provincial regulations, which are considered essentially humane. What sets organic butchering apart is the way in which the machinery is treated – for example the equipment must be disinfected following organic standards before the meat is cut.

Manufacturing meat products such as sausages or bacon also calls for organic measures. All of the curing must be done using organic ingredients and no artificial additives, preservatives or dyes are allowed in the final processing. The end result, such as the Wehrmanns' wild-boar prosciutto, can be sublime.

Fishing for organic foods

Organic fish and seafood are very rare and most certification bodies do not even have guidelines covering organic fish farming. However, biologist-cum-organic salmon farmer Ann Heath gets pretty animated when it comes to talking about Yellow Island Aquaculture Ltd., which she and her husband John run on Quadra Island in British Columbia. "It's the only organic Chinook salmon farm in the world, but it's not certified," she notes. But it isn't because the Heaths haven't been trying.

"We applied for certification five or six years ago but there were no certification standards for fish farming of any kind," Heath explains, "so we decided to write our own for BCARA" (the British Columbia Association for Regenerative Agriculture, one of the certifying bodies in the province). For years the Heaths have been waiting for BCARA to approve their proposed organic standards, which must provide assurances that the fish farm will not have an impact on other ocean activity or fish stocks. However, because these guidelines will probably set a precedent, Heath says "we'll wait until everybody is happy with the standards." In fact, these organic fish-farming standards could possibly cover other species of seafood such as trout, tilapia, eel and carp, says BCARA president Walter Kattenberg, who is working with the Heaths on the development of the standards.

There are some certified-organic seafood products such as dulse, kelp, nori and laver, which are available from Maine Coast Sea Vegetables in Franklin, Maine. In 1992, the company became the first processor worldwide to be certified for its harvesting and handling procedures of sea vegetables. Approximately 40,000 pounds (18,000 kilograms) of sea vegetables are harvested every year by the company.

Back on the West Coast, Yellow Island Aquaculture has been in operation for almost 14 years and Heath credits the farm's success to good husbandry and stock. "With any form of animal or plant, you have to treat it with care and keep it in optimal conditions. I love my critters and my fish are happy and we have one of the best sites in the world for Chinook salmon," she enthuses.

Quadra Island is sandwiched between Vancouver Island and the mainland, explains Heath, with the very turbulent Seymour Narrows at its shore. "The water quality is spectacular because of the volume of water that passes through the narrows. It never gets more than 13° C (56° F) or below 8° C (47° F), and the salinity never changes," she adds.

Similar to other organic farming, Yellow Island Aquaculture keeps its stock at a lower density than is the case with fish in commercial farms – five kilograms per cubic meter (11 pounds per 1.3 cubic yards). Each cage contains 1,000 cubic meters (1,300 cubic yards) but because Chinook salmon move in circles (which means that the corners of the cages aren't used), Heath says they calculate each cage as having only 750 cubic meters (975 cubic yards). The Heaths raise about 100,000 Chinook a year, harvesting every Wednesday for their local orders, and every four to six weeks for their orders in Ontario and Quebec.

The farm also has a hatchery that allows the Heaths more control over the health of their stock: "If you breed an animal that has never had an antibiotic, and its mother and grandmother has never had an antibiotic, then it is naturally more disease-resistant to start with." Although Heath claims she's not a marketing person, demand for Yellow Island's products has exceeded supply.

The clean, fresh taste of organic dairy foods

A breakthrough decision was celebrated by Canadian organic proponents and dairy lovers in 1995 when the Dairy Farmers of Ontario, which controls the marketing and distribution of milk in the province, finally allowed a group of organic milk producers to keep their product separate from the province-wide milk pool.

In January 1996, OntarBio Organic Farmers Co-op, a certified-organic farmer-run co-operative, debuted its Organic Meadow dairy products to the public. Since then, OntarBio has been gradually adding more products to its Organic Meadow line, with several types of milk, yogurt, butter and cheeses available in British Columbia, Ontario, Quebec and the Maritimes.

Dairy cows are raised and treated like other organically raised animals – without chemical hormones, antibiotics or genetically engineered products, nursed back to health using homeopathic treatments, fed organic grains and hay and set to pasture on fields free of pesticides and synthetic fertilizers.

And the clean organic taste shines through. The dairy products have a rich full flavor that comes in part from the Jersey and Brown Swiss herds, which have a higher butterfat and milk-solid content. On average, 70,000 liters (61,600 quarts) of milk are collected every two weeks from eight organic dairy farms.

In the United States, the largest certified-organic dairy is Organic Valley/Coulee Region Organic Produce Pool Cooperative based in La Farge, Wisconsin. The co-operative began about a decade ago with only a few Wisconsin farmers and has since grown into an award-winning, 150-farm operation.

Some of the co-operative's sales growth is due to the increasing concern over recombinant Bovine Growth Hormone (rBGH, also known as Bovine Somatotropin, BST) in American milk. This growth hormone is injected into the cow to increase milk production; however, it can have serious health effects on the animal and there is some concern as to its implications on human health as well. (Currently, rBGH is not registered for sale in Canada but the product is under discussion.) The co-operative also believes that as consumers become more informed and educated about corporate agribusiness, many of them actively seek out food from small family farms.

Uncorking organic wines

The designation of wines as organic can be confusing and misleading because while a vineyard might use organic fruit for its wine, its winemaking process might use chemical additives. A certified-organic wine, on the other hand, is one that is made with certified-organic fruit and is certified for its wine-making process, which must adhere to organic standards.

France and Germany lead the way in producing organic wines, but a growing number of vineyards in North America are now following suit. According to a September 1997 article in the *San Francisco*

Examiner, the organic-wine industry is growing 20 percent annually and now makes up 1 percent of the premium wine market in the United States. The paper also reported that winemakers predict that organic wines will make up half of the total wine market in 10 to 15 years.

Organic winemakers grow their fruit following the same practices and philosophies as other organic farmers and then keep their filtering and processing to a minimum. They also use minute amounts of sulfites – if any at all. (A small measure is allowed by most certification bodies.) Only naturally derived ingredients are allowed under the strict organic standards.

In 1995, Hainle Vineyards Estate Winery Ltd. in Peachland, B.C. became the first Canadian winery to be certified for its vineyard and winemaking. Sandra Hainle, marketing director and co-owner of the vineyard, says that the Okanagan climate is ideal for organic grape growing and others agree. Hainle Vineyards, which is co-owned by Sandra's husband Tilman (the estate's winemaker), has successfully encouraged some of its contracted grape growers to convert to organic practices and attain certification. In 1998, Hainle Vineyards will have released a dozen different certified-organic wines, the majority being sold in British Columbia with some going to Alberta and Ontario.

Another winery that is certified for both its vineyard and winemaking process is Hallcrest Vineyards in California, which sells its products under The Organic Wine Works label. The vineyard offers 11 certified-organic wines in the United States. Other Californian vineyards such as Fetzer Vineyards (probably the largest certified-organic wine grape grower in North America) and Frey Vineyards use organic grapes in some of their wines, but their winemaking is not certified. Check labels for a certification symbol or designation.

Organic beer makes some headway

Caps off to British Columbia's Pacific Western Brewing Co. (PWB) for releasing Canada's first certified-organic beer in November 1997. Bottled NatureLand Organic was launched simultaneously in Canada and Japan (under three different private labels). In April 1998, the beer also became available in draft form.

The Prince George-based brewery makes NatureLand Organic from certified-organic malt barley from Saskatchewan, certified-organic hops from Germany and Australia and the pure spring water that comes from directly underneath the brewery. Besides using organic ingredients, PWB must also produce the beer following organic-production standards, says marketing co-ordinator Greg Paolini.

The five percent-alcohol beer had an unprecedented response before its official launch, says PWB's president Kazuko Komatsu, with a large number of pre-orders from liquor stores, restaurants and hotels in British Columbia. "The organic designation is much more than a catchy name attached to a beer label," she emphasizes. "We began to research the brewing of a certified-organic product in 1992. It took some time to convince farmers to commit to the three full crop-year requirements," Komatsu adds. (This is the length of time the land and crops must be free of pesticides, chemical seed treatment, etc. to obtain organic certification.) The wait was worth it however, and Paolini says that another organic variety is already in the works.

Food for thought

For anyone who appreciates good, wholesome food, the importance of organic agriculture is immeasurable. And if you think about it, that alone is sufficient reason to support organic growers – by purchasing the fruits of their labor in stores, at their farms and local farmers' markets, through community shared agriculture programs and at restaurants that use organic ingredients. Encourage your local retailers to carry organic products and explain why. By using the information within these pages and using organic ingredients for the recipes, you will be making a difference to your health and the environment's. And better yet, you will be enjoying fresh, delicious food – food as it was meant to be.

ORGANIC SOURCES

Knives & Forks, Advocates for Organic Agriculture, produced this cookbook and organizes the annual Feast of Fields event in southern Ontario. Knives & Forks is a non-profit coalition of organic producers, environmentally concerned chefs and other food professionals, and enlightened consumers who are committed to raising the understanding and support for organic agriculture and environmental responsibility.

The organization's mandate is to promote awareness of the environmental and human benefits of organic agriculture; to increase both co-operation and market relationships between organic producers and interested food professionals and consumers; to establish links with other environmental organizations with the intention of furthering public awareness of the importance of organic agriculture; and to support organic projects and events. For more information call (416) 422-1944 or 1-800-719-9108.

WEBSITES

Here are some websites that focus on organic agriculture including good information on the proposed national standards in Canada and the United States and links to other sites such as stores that sell and farmers who grow organic food:

www.gks.com
Canada's master host of organic information with links to certified-organic growers and retailers across the country

www.gks.com/cog/
website for the Canadian Organic Growers★ includes articles from its publication, updates on organic news and links to non-governmental and governmental sites

www.alternatives.com/ffcf/
website for FarmFolk/CityFolk★ has excellent information and resources on organic agriculture and the environment and good links to other food and agriculture websites

www.gks.com/coab/
website of the Canadian Organic Advisory Board★ with details on the national organic standards and lists all of the organic certification bodies in Canada

www.organicfood.com
website of the Organic Trading and Information Center, which is dedicated to the growth of organic agriculture and helping consumers make informed choices; the site lists all of the organic certification bodies in the United States

www.ota.com
website for the Organic Trade Association, which educates North American consumers and legislators about organic agriculture and production

www.organic.pa.mb.ca
website for the Organic Producers Association of Manitoba with links to where to buy and eat organics

www.gks.com/efao/
website for the Ecological Farmers Association of Ontario, which has a mandate to communicate and share information about organic agriculture, includes upcoming farm tours and courses

www.gks.com/NSOGA/
website for the Nova Scotia Organic Growers Association★ includes sources, events, certification information and updates on the national organic standards

eap.mcgill.ca
website for Ecological Agriculture Projects★ offers many on-line resources and services

---

★ *See* Organizations, Canada (next page)

www.ams.usda.gov/nop
Agricultural Marketing Service website on U.S. Department of Agriculture's proposed national organic legislation

www.rain.org/~sals/my.html
website for the American-based Don't Panic Eat Organic, which has numerous links to other sites

www.mothers.org/mothers
website of American-based Mothers and Others for a Livable Planet, which promotes consumer choices that are safe and ecologically sustainable

web.iquest.net/ofma
website for the Organic Farmers Marketing Association in the United States, which provides public education and information on organic farming and resources

sunsite.unc.edu/farming-connection
website for the American-based Sustainable Farming Connection with information on organic agriculture and links to other organic organizations

www.ecoweb.dk/ifoam
website for the International Federation of Organic Agricultural Movements (IFOAM), a worldwide umbrella group with more than 600 member organizations in 95 countries

www.yahoo.com/Business_and_Economy/Companies/Food/Natural_Organic/
international list of organic businesses, manufacturers and stores that sell organic food and links to their sites

envirolink.org
"The largest online environmental information resource on the planet."

www.webdirectory.com
an international directory of environmental research sources and groups with a search engine

www.wildoats.com
website for Wild Oats Market, Inc. (see U.S. stores) has links to manufacturers and processors of organic foods

www.wholefoods.com
website for Whole Foods Market (see U.S. stores) has links to manufacturers and processors of organic foods

www.hainle.com
website for Hainle Vineyards Estate Winery in British Columbia, which includes in-depth information about organic winemaking and wines, as well as recipes and an extensive links page

www.isgnet.com/ogwa
website for California-based Organic Grapes into Wine Alliance, which provides information on organic winemaking and wines, production standards and lists its current members with links to their websites

ORGANIZATIONS

Here is a short list of groups that can provide information on organic agriculture and where to buy organic food.

CANADA

The **Canadian Organic Growers (COG)** is a national non-profit educational group with several chapters across the country. COG publishes a quarterly newsletter and the *Organic Resource Guide,* a national directory of organic retailers, farmers and other useful contacts. The chapters are great contacts for local sources and information on organics. To become a member, contact Kathy Lamarche, R.R. 2, Almonte, Ont., K0A 1A0 (613) 256-1848; fax (613) 256-4453. For other information, visit their website at www.gks.com/cog/ or contact a chapter near you:

COG Alberta, Cathy Taylor, 1124-4th Ave. NE, Calgary, Alta., T2E 0K5 (403) 263-9941; fax (403)291-9049

COG BC Islands, Elizabeth White, 171 Vesuvius Bay Rd., Salt Spring Island, B.C., V8K 1K3 (250) 537-2616; fax (250) 537-2681

COG Durham, Judy Hurvid, R.R. 1, 4636 - #2, Newtonville, Ont., L0A 1J0 (905) 786-2089; fax (905) 434-4608

COG Essex-Kent, Francine DeMeyer, 26933 Winterline Rd., R.R. 6, Wallaceburg, Ont., N8A 4L3 (519) 354-7675; fax (519) 687-3745

COG Kawartha, Brenda Coons, 1910 Television Rd., Peterborough, Ont., K9L 1E9 (705) 748-0046; fax (705) 745-4413

COG Niagara, Laura Sabourin, 3403 - 11th St. Louth, R.R. 1, St. Catharines, Ont., L2R 6P7 (905) 562-0151; fax (905) 562-0152

COG Perth-Waterloo-Wellington, Audrey Fyfe, R.R. 2, Drayton, Ont., N0G 1P0 (519) 669-3700

COG South Island, Mary Alice Johnson, Box 807, Sooke, B.C., V0S 1N0 (250) 642-3671

COG Toronto, Randall J. Fox, 18 Grenville St., #1502, Toronto, Ont., M4Y 3B3 (416) 922-5523; website: www.gks.com/cog/toronto/

COG Wentworth-Burlington, Ursula Brown, 845 Collinson Rd., R.R. 2, Dundas, Ont., L9H 5E2 (905) 627-7651

Canadian Health Food Association

Serge Lavoie, 550 Alden Rd, Suite 205, Markham, Ont., L3R 6A8 1 (800) 661-4510; (416) 479-6939; fax (416) 479-1516 National trade association focusing on health and organic food

Canadian Organic Advisory Board

c/o Dr. Robert McDonald, CEO, 610, 910-7 Ave. SW, Calgary, Alta., T2P 3N8 (403) 266-1122; fax (403) 261-3955; website: www.gks.com/coab/ This charitable organization is committed to the establishment of a national Canadian organic standard that will help protect and promote the Canadian organic industry at home and abroad.

Earth to Table

#201, 917 18th Ave. SW, Calgary, Alta., T2T 0H2 (403) 244-6071; fax (403) 266-4055 This coalition of chefs, growers, distributors and consumers promotes sustainable food choices to achieve a future with food security and raises the understanding and support for locally and organically grown products. The group's members exchange resources and ideas, promote the use of fresh local foods within the industry and strengthen the bond between earth and table.

Eco-Farm & Garden, Elizabeth Irving Box 15, Oxford Mills, Ont., K0G 1S0 (613) 258-4045; fax (613) 258-0542 New organic publication created from merging Canadian Organic Growers' *Cognition* with Resource Efficient Agricultural Production's *Sustainable Farming*

Ecological Agricultural Projects

McGill University (Macdonald Campus), 21, 111 Lakeshore Rd., Ste-Anne-de-Bellevue, Que., H9X 3V9 (514) 398-7771; fax (514) 398-7621; e-mail: info@eap.mcgill.ca; website: eap.mcgill.ca EAP's mission is to facilitate the establishment of food systems that are nutritionally sound, socially just, humane, economically viable and environmentally sustainable. EAP provides information on community shared agriculture and has a list of farmers participating in CSA programs across Canada.

FarmFolk/CityFolk

#208, 2211 W. 4th Ave., Vancouver, B.C., V6K 1S2 (604) 730-0450; e-mail: farmcity@alternatives.com; website: www.alternatives.com/ffcf/ A not-for-profit registered charity that strives to reduce the distance between field and table; reintegrate urban and rural concerns; utilize a holistic approach to the regeneration of community; and develop and maintain a just and sustainable food system. Focusing on food, environment, health and agriculture, FarmFolk/CityFolk organizes the Feast of Fields in Vancouver, presents regular festivals and forums, conducts research and participates in policy making. Its excellent website has a wealth of information, resources and links to other food and agriculture sites.

Field to Table

200 Eastern Ave., Toronto, Ont., M5A 1J1 (416) 363-6441; fax (416) 392-6650; e-mail: fdshare@web.net Field to Table, part of Foodshare Metro Toronto, runs the Organic Food Box program in the Toronto region

Nova Scotia Organic Growers Association

Box 16, Annapolis Royal, N.S., B0S 1A0 (902) 825-6209; website: www.gks.com/NSOGA/ A group of farmers, gardeners, consumers, environmentalists, scientists, educators and health practitioners who promote wholesome food, sustainable communities and wise stewardship of the earth. NSOGA maintains an organic certification program and conducts research into sustainable farming. It also publishes *Organic Times* and holds several workshops and events a year.

OPIS - Organic Product Information Service, Mark Gimby, 15 Innovation Blvd., Saskatoon, Sask., S7N 2X8 (306) 933-5449; fax (306) 933-7896 Saskatchewan Research Council-sponsored organic brokerage-clearing house

Organic Conference at University of Guelph, Tomás Nimmo, Box 116, Collingwood, Ont., L9Y 3Z4 (705) 444-0923; fax (705) 444-0380; e-mail: organix@georgian.net Canada's largest annual organic farming conference

Pro Organics Marketing Inc., Debra Boyle,
3454 Lougheed Hwy., Vancouver, B.C., V5M 2A4
(604) 253-6549; fax (604) 253-0439;
e-mail: prosales@proorganics.com
Unit #3-5, Building 709, 433 Horner Ave., Etobicoke,
Ont., M8W 4Y4 (416) 252-3386; fax (416) 252-3142;
e-mail: mfronte@proorganics.com
Canada's leading organic produce importer and distributor

Rare Breeds Canada, Dan Price-Jones,
Trent University, Environmental & Resource Study
Program, Peterborough, Ont., K9J 7B8
(613) 473-1395; fax (613) 473-1396
Promotes and preserves rare farm livestock and poultry

Seeds of Diversity Canada, Garrett Pittenger,
16812 Humber Stn. Rd., R.R. 3, Caledon, Ont.,
L0N 1E0 (905) 880-4848; fax (905) 880-0123;
website: www.interlog.com/~sodc
Promotes conservation, preservation and enhancement of
endangered seeds and plants and runs a seed exchange for
members; runs a Knives & Forks-funded garlic program,
which researches and maintains heirloom varieties

WWOOF-Canada, John Vanden Heuve,
R.R. 2 Carlson Rd., S-18, C9, Nelson, B.C., V1L 5P5
(250) 354-4417; fax c/o (250) 352-3927
Willing Workers On Organic Farms is a unique international program that organizes apprentices to work
on organic farms

UNITED STATES

Alternative Farming Systems Information
Room 304, National Agricultural Library, 10301
Baltimore, Beltsville, Md., 20705-2351
(301) 504-6425; fax (301) 504-6409;
e-mail: san@nal.usda.gov; website:
www.ces.ncsu.edu/san/htdocs/events (allows users to
add events to the site)
A leading international database of organic events and
contacts

Chefs Collaborative 2000
Oldways Preservation & Exchange Trust, 25 First St.,
Cambridge, Mass., 02141
(617) 621-3000; fax (617) 621-1230; website:
www.chefnet.com/cc2000
A non-profit membership organization of about 1,500
chefs across the United States that promotes sustainable cuisine by teaching children, supporting local
farmers, educating each other and inspiring customers
to choose good, clean food. With 25 local chapters, it
runs the Adopt-A-School Program and organizes an
annual retreat for its members.

Community Alliance with Family Farmers
Box 363, Davis, Calif., 95617
(530) 756-8518X17; fax (530) 756-7857; website:
www.caff.org
Publishes the *National Organic Directory*, a resource
guide that includes growers, wholesalers, retailers and
organic businesses throughout North America; website
has links to CSAs and farmers' markets in California

CSA Network
130 Ruckytucks Rd., Stillwater, N.Y., 12170
(518) 583-4613
A community shared agriculture group

Institute for Alternative Agriculture
9200 Edmonston Rd., Suite 117, Greenbelt, Md.,

20770-1551 (301) 441-8777; fax (301) 220-0164
A major U.S. organic alternative promotion and
research group

Seeds of Change
P.O. Box 15700, Sante Fe, N.M., 87506
website: www.seedsofchange.com
Seeds of Change offers a selection of certified-organic,
open-pollinated seeds — many of which are heirloom,
rare and traditional varieties — of vegetables, herbs and
flowers; Deep Diversity, a seed bank that is owned and
operated by Seeds of Change, has more than 1,000
varieties of seeds

Upper Midwest Organic Conference
N7834 County Road B, Spring Valley, Wis., 54767
(715) 772-6819; fax (715) 772-3153;
e-mail: fjeoc@win.bright.net
One of the largest organic conferences in the U.S.

RETAIL OUTLETS - CANADA

BRITISH COLUMBIA
Capers Markets
1675 Robson St., Vancouver, B.C., V6G 1C8
(604) 687-5288
2285 W. 4th Ave., Vancouver, B.C., V6K 1N9
(604) 739-6676
2496 Marine Dr., West Vancouver, B.C., V7V 1L1
(604) 925-3316

Choices
2627 W. 16th Ave., Vancouver, B.C., V6K 3C2
(604) 736-0009

Circling Dawn Organic Foods
1045 Commercial Dr., Vancouver, B.C., V5L 3X1
(604) 255-2326

East End Food Co-op
1034 Commercial Dr., Vancouver, B.C., V5L 3W9
(604) 254-5044

East Vancouver Farmers' Market
(Sat., 9 a.m.- 2 p.m., mid-May to Thanksgiving weekend)
Trout Lake Community Centre, 15th Avenue and
Victoria Street, Vancouver, B.C.

ALBERTA
Community Natural Foods
1304 -10 Ave. SW, Calgary, Alta., T3C 0J2
(403) 229-2383

Harvest Sun Whole Foods
303 -19th St. SW, Calgary, Alta., T2N 2J2
(403) 270-8433; fax (403) 270-7294

Options
126 - 513 8th Ave. SW, Calgary, Alta., T2P 1G3
(403) 265-9483; fax (403) 265-9473

Terra Natural Food Market
10313 82 Ave., Edmonton, Alta., T6E 1Z9
(403) 433-6807

SASKATCHEWAN
Old Fashion Foods
501 Victoria Ave., Regina, Sask., S4N 0P8
(306) 352-8623

Saskatoon Herbs & Health
#3-1005 Broadway Ave., Saskatoon, Sask., S7N 1C1
(306) 664-1070

Sunlite Health Foods
1308 Central Ave., Prince Albert, Sask., S6V 4W3
(306) 922-4372

MANITOBA
Harvest Collective
877 Westminster Ave., Winnipeg, Man., R3G 1B3
(204) 772-4359; fax (204) 475-1462
664 Corydon Ave., Winnipeg, Man., R3M 0X7
(204) 475-1459; fax (204) 475-1462
Stone Ground Daily Bread
1399 Pembina Hwy., Winnipeg, Man., R3T 2B8
(204) 474-5900
Tall Grass Prairie Bread Co.
859 Westminster Ave., Winnipeg, Man., R3G 1B1
(204) 783-5097

ONTARIO
Alternatives
579 Kerr St., Oakville, Ont., L6K 3E1 (905) 844-2375
Baldwin Natural Foods
20fi Baldwin St., Toronto, Ont., M5T 1L2
(416) 979-1777
The Big Carrot
348 Danforth Ave., Toronto, Ont., M4K 1N8
(416) 466-2129
Danfield's Organic Market
150 Dundas St., London, Ont., N6A 1G1
(519) 744-5331
Eating Well Organically
104 King St. S., Waterloo, Ont., N2J 1P5 (519) 883-0734
**Eternal Abundance Organic and Natural Food
Store** 3066 Bloor St. W., Etobicoke, Ont., M8X 1C4
(416) 234-5258
Full Circle Natural Foods
68 Queen St. S., Kitchener, Ont., N2G 1V6
(519) 744-5331
Haedae Farms
Farm store: 9121 Peterson Rd., Addison, Ont.,
K0E 1A0   (613) 924-2052; fax (613) 924-9755
also opening a store in Merrickville on the main street
(613) 269-4330
Harmony Whole Foods
163 First St., Unit A, Credit Creek North,
Orangeville, Ont., L9W 3J9   (519) 941-8961
Karma Co-op
739 Palmerston Ave., Toronto, Ont., M6G 2R3
(416) 534-1470
Noah's Natural Foods
2395 Yonge St., Toronto, Ont., M4P 3E7 (416) 488-0904
322 Bloor St. W., Toronto, Ont., M5S 1W5 (416) 968-7930
Ottawa Organic Farmers' Market
(Saturdays, 10 a.m. to 2 p.m.) Kingsway United
Church, 630 Island Park Drive, Ottawa, Ont., K1Y 0B7
Rainbow Natural Foods
Britannia Shopping Plaza, 1487 Richmond Rd.,
Ottawa, Ont., K2B 6R9   (613) 726-9200
Shisko's Country Produce
605 Halls Road South, Whitby, Ont., L1N 5R4
(905) 430-7672
THE Organic Farmers' Market
(Saturdays 8 a.m. to 2 p.m.) Mirvish Village, Markham
Street south of Bloor Street West, Toronto, Ont.
True Food
239 Lakeshore Rd. E., Mississauga, Ont., L5G 1G8
(905) 274-3035; fax (905) 274-3195
Vegetable Kingdom
443 Adelaide St. W., Toronto, Ont., M5V 1S9
(416) 703-6447

The Village Market
(Saturdays 9 a.m. to 1 p.m.)
Toronto Waldorf School, 9100 Bathurst St., Thornhill,
Ont., L4C 8C7   (905) 707-5771
The Wholesome Food Store
2238 Queen St. E., Toronto, Ont., M4E 1A2
(416) 690-9500

QUEBEC
Club Organic
4341 rue Frontenac, Montréal, Que., H2H 2M4
(514) 523-0223; fax (514) 523-0216
Optimum Natural Foods
630, Sherbrooke ouest, #100, Montréal, Que.,
H3A 1E4   (514) 845-1015
Sesame Natural Foods
5550, Sherbrooke ouest, Montréal, Que., H4H 1W3
(514) 488-9886
Tau
4238, rue St-Denis, Montréal, Que., H2J 2K8
(514) 843-4420

NEW BRUNSWICK
Aura Whole Foods
207 Charlotte St., Fredericton, N.B., E3B 1L5
(506) 454-4240
Jacob's Larder
38 York St., Sackville, N.B., E4L 4R4 (506) 536-2303

NOVA SCOTIA
EOS Fine Foods
10 Front St., Wolfville, N.S., B0P 1X0 (902) 542-7103
Great Ocean Natural Foods
6485 Quinpool Rd., Halifax, N.S., B3L 1B2
(902) 425-7400; fax (902) 425-7402
Sunflower Natural Foods
194 Main St., Antigonish, N.S., B2G 2L6 (902) 863-1194
Super Natural Foods
1505 Barrington St., Halifax, N.S., B3J 3K5
(902) 423-8630

PRINCE EDWARD ISLAND
The Root Cellar
34 Queen St., Charlottetown, P.E.I., C1A 4A3
(902) 892-6227

RETAIL OUTLETS - U.S.A.
*Due to the number of stores carrying organic food in the
United States, we have only listed the two national natural-
and organic-food chains. For other organic retailers across the
country, check out the Community Alliance with Family
Farmers' National Organic Directory or visit one of the
websites listed at the beginning of this section that provide links
to stores.*

Whole Foods Market operates stores under the names
**Whole Foods Market, Bread & Circus, Fresh
Fields, Wellspring Grocery and Merchant of Vino**
Head Office, 601 North Lamar, Suite 300, Austin, Tex.,
78703 (512) 477-4455; fax (512) 477-1301; website:
www.wholefoods.com (lists all of the store locations)
Wild Oats Market Inc. operates stores under the
names **Wild Oats Market, Alfalfa's Markets, Capers
Markets, Oasis Fine Foods and Sunshine Grocer**
Head Office, 1645 Broadway, Boulder, Col., 80302
(303) 440-5220; fax (303) 440-5280; e-mail:
info@wildoats.com; website: www.wildoats.com (lists
all of the store locations)

APPETIZERS

Serves 4

TEA-SCENTED GOAT CHEESE

You can impress your guests with just two ingredients! Chèvre marinated in tisane, jasmine or Earl Grey would go well with fruit, while the nutty flavor of Genmai Cha or the smoky flavor of Lapsang Souchong would be great in a salad.

The highest quality teas contain only the leaf buds and the top two leaves of the plant; the lower leaves are used in lower quality teas. These leaves can all be used for black, green and oolong teas: black tea, which dominates the tea market, is fermented; green tea is unfermented and oolong tea is partially fermented.

CHEESECLOTH

1	round soft unripened goat cheese (about 4 oz [125 g])	1
2 tbsp	flavored tea (such as fruit tisane, Lapsang Souchong, Genmai Cha, jasmine tea, etc.)	25 mL

1. Wrap cheese in a single layer of cheesecloth with very little overlap.

2. On a piece of plastic wrap large enough to wrap the cheese, spread 1 tbsp (15 mL) of the tea in a band lengthwise down the middle of the plastic wrap. Place the curved edge of the cheese in the tea at one end of the wrap and tightly roll the cheese in the wrap, making sure that the tea is covering the side of the cheese all the way around. Place the cheese with one of the flat sides up and sprinkle half the remaining tea over the cheese. Close the end tightly. Repeat on the remaining side. You should end up with a piece of cheese that is almost completely covered in tea, tightly wrapped in plastic.

3. Refrigerate for 24 hours. (Keep in mind that the longer the cheese is marinated, the stronger the flavor of the tea.)

4. Remove the plastic wrap and cheesecloth from the cheese and serve.

FROM THE KITCHEN OF
KAREN BARNABY

RED LENTIL HUMMUS

Makes 2 cups (500 mL)

1 cup	red lentils, rinsed	250 mL
5	cloves garlic	5
2 tsp	ground cumin	10 mL
1 tbsp	chopped fresh basil	15 mL
1/4 cup	yellow (or red) sun-dried tomatoes	50 mL
1/2 cup	olive oil	125 mL
	Salt and pepper	

1. In a saucepan cover lentils with 4 cups (1 L) salted water; bring to a boil. Reduce heat and cook for 30 minutes or until tender; drain.

2. In a food processor, combine lentils with garlic, cumin, basil, sun-dried tomatoes and olive oil; purée until smooth. Season to taste with salt and pepper. Serve with Chef Ennest's FLATBREAD *(see recipe, page 151).*

This is an unusual and delicious interpretation of the very popular chickpea hummus. It's an easy recipe that is not only a favorite with the River Café's customers but with the staff as well. The kitchen notes that before serving the hummus, it must be tasted to adjust the seasonings – which allows the cook a chance to enjoy some before all the guests dig in.

FROM THE KITCHEN OF
DWAYNE ENNEST

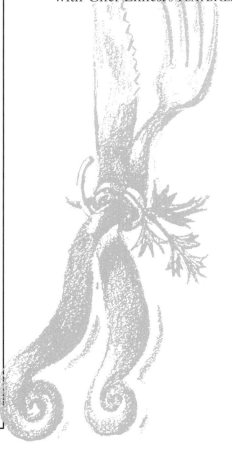

PARMIGIANO-REGGIANO AND FRESH BASIL GÂTEAU

Serves 8

This delicious appetizer is definitely not for people watching their cholesterol — but it's really not as rich as it sounds.

The name Parmigiano-Reggiano is strictly protected by law and only the cheese that comes from particular areas of northern Italy can bear its name. It is more expensive than other parmesan cheeses (the generic name for the hard, granular cheese) such as Padano and Romano, but many consider the cheese worth it. Chunks of Parmesan are recommended over the pre-grated version as freshly grated Parmesan tastes much better and it keeps well in the refrigerator.

PREHEAT OVEN TO 325° F (160° C)

8-INCH (20 CM) SPRINGFORM PAN LINED WITH PLASTIC WRAP

I cup	ricotta	250 mL
I cup	cream cheese	250 mL
I cup	freshly grated Parmigiano-Reggiano	250 mL
3	eggs	3
2	cloves garlic	2
	Juice of 3 lemons	
I tbsp	flour	15 mL
2 tbsp	melted butter	25 mL
	Salt and pepper to taste	
Pinch	freshly grated nutmeg	Pinch
3 cups	basil leaves, washed and dried	750 mL
I cup	sour cream	250 mL
4 to 6	vine-ripened tomatoes, sliced	4 to 6
	Extra virgin olive oil	
	Toasted pine nuts	

1. In a food processor, combine ricotta, cream cheese and Parmigiano-Reggiano; process until smooth. Add eggs, garlic, lemon juice, flour, butter, salt, pepper and nutmeg. Process until combined. Add basil leaves and process well. Add sour cream and process until just blended. Pour into prepared springform pan and bake for 50 minutes.

2. Remove from pan and allow to cool for at least 6 hours. To serve, slice with a hot knife and serve on a slice of vine-ripened tomato drizzled with extra virgin olive oil and sprinkled with toasted pine nuts.

FROM THE KITCHEN OF
CHARLES PART

MUSHROOM CROSTINI

Serves 6 to 8

Here is a quick guide to help you identify the mushrooms in this recipe:

Oyster: *ivory to taupe color; softly lobed and fan-shaped; grows in delicate overlapping clusters*

Chanterelle: *gold to orange color; trumpet-shaped, tapering down to the stem; soft*

Portobello: *cream to tan color; large; wide, flat cap; firm*

Porcini: *brownish; puffy, round cap on a bulbous stem; smooth and firm*

Button: *these are the common white mushrooms*

FROM THE KITCHEN OF
GLENN MCIVOR

PREHEAT OVEN TO 375° F (190° C)
BAKING SHEET

1	baguette cut diagonally into 1/2-inch (1 cm) slices	1
	Smoke oil *or* olive oil for brushing	
1/4 cup	olive oil	50 mL
8 oz	oyster mushrooms, cleaned and sliced	250 g
8 oz	chanterelle mushrooms, cleaned and sliced	250 g
8 oz	portobello mushrooms, cleaned and sliced	250 g
8 oz	porcini mushrooms, cleaned and sliced	250 g
8 oz	button mushrooms, cleaned and sliced	250 g
1 tbsp	chopped garlic	15 mL
1/4 cup	dry white wine	50 mL
1/4 cup	chopped parsley	50 mL
4 cups	whipping (35%) cream	1 L
	Salt and pepper to taste	
1/4 cup	grated Parmesan	50 mL

1. Place cut bread on a baking sheet and brush with smoke oil. Bake in preheated oven for 12 to 15 minutes, until crisp. Set aside.

2. In a skillet, heat olive oil over medium heat. Add all mushrooms and sauté until softened; drain excess liquid. Add garlic, wine and three-quarters of the parsley; simmer for 15 minutes. Add whipping cream; increase heat and cook, stirring constantly, 15 minutes until reduced. Season to taste with salt and pepper; add Parmesan cheese. Spoon onto toasts and sprinkle with the remaining parsley.

BASMATI RICE CRACKER WITH GREEN OLIVE-CORIANDER TAPENADE

Serves 6

PREHEAT OVEN TO 375° F (190° C)

BAKING SHEET, OILED

CRACKER

4 oz	butter	125 g
1/4 cup	finely diced shallots	50 mL
4	cloves garlic, finely minced	4
1/2 tsp	saffron	2 mL
1	bay leaf	1
2 1/2 cups	chicken stock *or* vegetable stock	625 mL
2 cups	basmati rice, rinsed	500 mL

TAPENADE

2	bunches coriander, washed well	2
1 tbsp	green peppercorns	15 mL
1 cup	large green olives, pitted	250 mL
2	cloves garlic, finely minced	2
1 tbsp	minced shallots	15 mL
1/2 cup	tomato concassé (about 2 medium tomatoes)	125 mL
1/2 cup	extra virgin olive oil	125 mL

1. Cracker: Melt 1 tbsp (15 mL) of the butter in a skillet over medium heat. Add shallots and garlic; cook until translucent, being careful not to burn the garlic. Add saffron, bay leaf and stock; bring to a boil. Add rice, stir and reduce the heat to low; simmer 15 to 20 minutes or until all the liquid has evaporated. Remove from heat, cover and let stand 25 minutes. Stir in remaining butter and allow to cool. Fluff with a fork.

2. Spoon out all rice mixture onto a sheet of plastic wrap. Cover with another sheet. With the other sheet (or with your hands), flatten into a rectangle about 1/8 inch (2 mm) thick. Cut into triangles and place on prepared baking sheet. Bake in preheated oven for 15 to 20 minutes or until crisp.

Chef Mandato serves grilled yellowfin tuna with this appetizer, but it also works well on its own.

Coriander is also known as cilantro or Chinese parsley and the Chinese call it "fragrant greens." The herb resembles flat-leaf parsley — but with finer, more delicate leaves — and a completely different flavor that people either love or hate. It is widely used in Latin America and Asia (Thais even use the roots).

For directions on how to make tomato concassé, see SPAGHETTI D'ESTATE (recipe, page 135).

FROM THE KITCHEN OF
MICHAEL MANDATO

3. Tapenade: In a pot of boiling water; blanch coriander for 1 minute. Refresh in ice water; drain. Transfer to a blender or food processor along with peppercorns and olives; purée.

4. In a bowl stir together coriander-olive mixture, garlic, shallots, tomato concassé and olive oil. Spoon onto cooled crackers and serve.

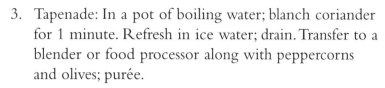

Organic FACTS

Organic farmers often control their pest problems by attracting beneficial wildlife to eat the pests. Multi-compartment martin houses, for example, can draw a colony of hundreds of insect-eating purple martins – that's a lot of bugs eliminated. Hedgerows, on the other hand, not only attract beneficial wildlife but also protect the land from soil erosion by acting as wind barriers. Another popular practice is companion planting – growing certain flowers or plants such as marigolds, nasturtiums and tansy to repel or lure pests.

GOAT CHEESE WITH SUN-DRIED TOMATOES ON PUFF PASTRY

Serves 4 to 6

Puff pastry is a buttery, flaky pastry that can be bought fresh or frozen. As its name implies, the pastry puffs up to about 8 times its original height. Some tips for working with puff pastry: for flakier results, work with chilled pastry in a cool area on a cool surface; lightly dust work surface and use a sharp knife, cutter or pastry wheel to prevent pulling or tearing; if possible, scallop the edges to help the pastry rise up straighter when it's baking; chill the cut pastry before baking to avoid shrinkage; and preheat the oven for at least 30 minutes.

PREHEAT OVEN TO 400° F (200° C)

8 oz	goat cheese	250 g
2 oz	sun-dried tomatoes (about 1/2 cup [125 mL]), sliced	50 g
1	shallot, minced	1
Half	bunch chives	Half
2 tbsp	virgin olive oil	25 mL
	Salt and pepper	
8 oz	puff pastry	250 g

1. In a bowl, combine goat cheese, sun-dried tomatoes, shallot, chives and olive oil. Add salt and pepper to taste.

2. Roll the puff pastry to about 1/8-inch (2 mm) thickness. Cut into 2-inch (5 cm) circles, preferably using a scalloped-edge cutter. Bake pastry in preheated oven for about 15 minutes or until brown and puffed up. Top with a spoonful of cheese mixture and serve.

Variation

The puff-pastry rounds can also be stuffed. Carefully cut the rounds into 2 layers. Place a spoonful of cheese mixture on bottom layer and cover with the top layer.

FROM THE KITCHEN OF
PAUL BOEHMER

Serves 4

SMOKED BLACK COD CARPACCIO ROLLED AROUND A BREAD STICK

*C*hef Couton smokes his black cod over maple and then slices it very thinly. (Carpaccio, in this instance, are transparently thin slices of fish, not beef.) If you can't find sliced smoked cod, freeze about 1 oz (25 g) smoked black cod for 24 hours and then slice it with a very sharp knife for the same results. Chef Couton serves this dish with a wild-mushroom bread stick, but feel free to use whatever accompaniment appeals to you.

SMOKED COD

1 tbsp	lime juice	15 mL
2 tbsp	olive oil	25 mL
8	thin slices smoked black cod	8

ROUILLE

1	small potato, peeled and chopped	1
Half	small red bell pepper, cut into quarters	Half
1/4 cup	olive oil	50 mL

GARNISH

1 tbsp	finely chopped red onion	15 mL
1 tbsp	finely chopped red bell pepper	15 mL
1 tbsp	finely chopped green pepper	15 mL
1 tbsp	finely chopped dill	15 mL
8	bread sticks	8

1. Cod: Whisk together lime juice and 2 tbsp (25 mL) olive oil; drizzle over smoked cod slices and set aside.

2. *Rouille:* Place potato and the quartered red pepper in a small pot and cover with water. Cook 10 minutes or until potato is tender; drain. Transfer to a food processor or blender; purée until smooth. Stir in 1/4 cup (50 mL) olive oil.

3. Garnish: Add chopped red onion, red and green peppers and dill to the *rouille*. Spread some of the *rouille*-garnish mixture on top of a cod slice and roll it around a bread stick.

FROM THE KITCHEN OF
FREDERIC COUTON

Serves 6

BLUE POTATO CROQUETTES WITH CHUNKY APPLE-APPLE SAGE SAUCE

Sage leaves are long and narrow with a downy texture. The herb is popular and native to the Mediterranean, where it is used to counterbalance rich and heavy foods. Use sage in moderation as it has a pungent, camphor-like flavor; purple and apple sage are less intense than common sage.

For directions on roasting garlic, see SMOKED BACON GRIDDLE CAKE (recipe, page 110).

HERBED CORNMEAL

1 cup	cornmeal	250 mL
1/2 cup	sunflower seeds	125 mL
1 tbsp	dried oregano	15 mL
1 tsp	dried thyme	5 mL
1/4 tsp	salt	1 mL
1/8 tsp	pepper	0.5 mL

CROQUETTES

4	medium new blue (or white) potatoes, boiled and mashed	4
1/2 tsp	finely chopped Thai chili peppers	2 mL
1 tbsp	finely chopped onion	15 mL
1 tbsp	chopped purple sage	15 mL
2 tbsp	lemon juice	25 mL
1	egg	1
2	cloves garlic, roasted and puréed	2
1/2 tsp	salt	2 mL
	Butter *or* oil for frying	

1. In a food processor, blend herbed cornmeal ingredients until very fine.

2. Beat croquette ingredients together and form into desired shape (about 1 1/2 tbsp [20 mL] per croquette). Roll croquettes in the herbed cornmeal mixture.

3. In a skillet, heat butter over medium heat and fry croquettes about 5 minutes on each side until golden brown. (Alternatively, deep-fry croquettes: whisk together 2 eggs and 1/2 cup (125 mL) milk; dip breaded croquettes in the egg-milk mixture, roll again in herbed cornmeal and set aside for about 1 hour in the refrigerator. Deep-fry until golden brown in a deep fryer at 350° F [180° C], about 5 minutes.)

4. Serve with CHUNKY APPLE-APPLE SAGE SAUCE (recipe follows).

FROM THE KITCHEN OF
MELVA BUELL AND
JACKIE MACKAY

CHUNKY APPLE-APPLE SAGE SAUCE

MAKES 1 CUP (250 ML)

3	medium apples, peeled, cored and cut into large chunks	3
1/4 cup	brown sugar	50 mL
1/4 cup	granulated sugar	50 mL
1 tbsp	chopped apple sage *or* 1 tsp (5 mL) regular sage	15 mL
1/2 cup	water	125 mL

1. In a saucepan combine all ingredients and bring to a boil. Reduce heat and simmer until apples are soft.

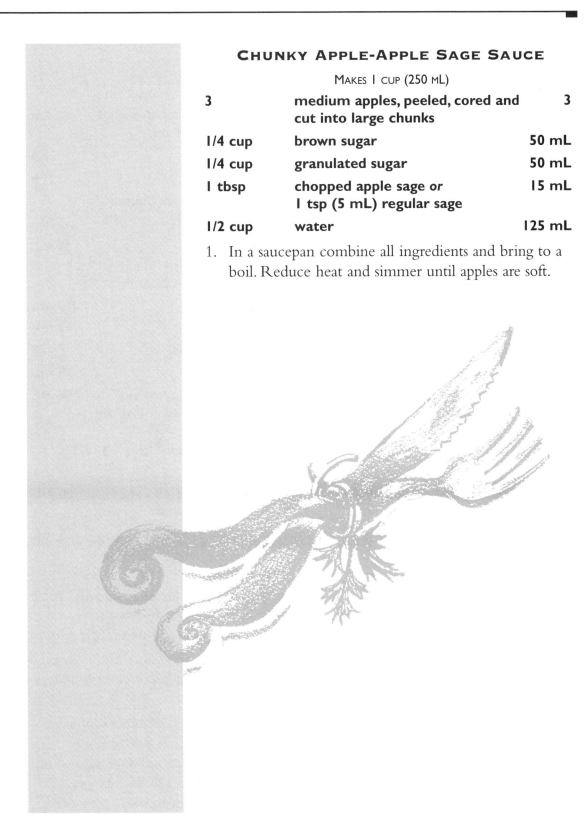

Serves 6

MAKI ROLL OF GRILLED QUAIL

PREHEAT BARBECUE OR GRILL

BAMBOO SUSHI MAT (OR A CLEAN DISH TOWEL)

6	large quail, butterflied, deboned with legs intact, skin on	6
6	Thai basil leaves	6
6	mint leaves	6
	Salt and crushed black pepper	
	Vegetable oil	
3 tbsp	oyster sauce	45 mL

MUSHROOM RAGOUT

1 cup	balsamic vinegar	250 mL
1/4 cup	sugar	50 mL
3	cloves garlic, slivered	3
2 tsp	vegetable oil	25 mL
3 cups	mushrooms (shiitake, oyster, cremini, etc.), cleaned and sliced	750 mL

MAKI ROLL

6	toasted *nori* sheets	6
2 cups	jasmine rice, cooked and kept warm 15 minutes before serving	500 mL
2 tbsp	toasted sesame seeds	25 mL
1	bunch snowpea leaves (or arugula or young spinach)	1
1	roasted pepper, peeled and seeded cut into 12 strips lengthwise	1

1. Lay quail flat on work surface. Gently place 1 basil leaf and 1 mint leaf between the skin and the breast. Season generously with salt and black pepper. Keep refrigerated until ready to grill.

2. Brush preheated grill with oil. Grill quail skin-side down, about 3 minutes; turn and cook another 3 minutes. (Actual cooking time will depend on size.) Brush liberally with oyster sauce. When cooked, remove quail from grill and cut in half lengthwise.

*N*ori *(seaweed paper) tastes best when lightly toasted. This can be done a few ways: Place on a cookie sheet and bake at 350° F (180° C) for 1 to 2 minutes or until it is crisp; or, using tongs, hold the* nori *over a flame; or put on a grill for 1 to 2 minutes, flip and toast the other side.* Nori *and bamboo sushi mats can be purchased in many Asian stores; some health-food stores also sell* nori.

For directions on deboning quail, see SALAD WITH GRILLED QUAIL (recipe, page 72). For directions on roasting a pepper, see ANTIPASTO MARINARA (recipe, page 38).

FROM THE KITCHEN OF
RENÉE FOOTE

3. Mushroom ragout: In a small saucepan, combine balsamic vinegar, sugar and garlic; bring to a boil and reduce until thick and syrupy. In another saucepan, heat vegetable oil over medium heat. Add mushrooms and sauté for 5 minutes or until almost cooked. Stir in balsamic reduction and cook another 5 to 10 minutes or until thick and sticky. Allow to cool.

4. Maki roll: Lay sheet of toasted *nori* on a bamboo sushi mat (or clean dish towel). On the longest width, place a layer of jasmine rice over the *nori*, leaving a 1/2-inch (1 cm) space at the far end. (Moisten your hands with water or rice vinegar if the rice is too sticky to handle.) Sprinkle generously with sesame seeds and place snowpea leaves on top.

5. In the center of these layers place 2 roasted red pepper strips and 1 tbsp (15 mL) mushroom ragout. Add quail so that quail legs are at opposite ends of the *nori*.

6. Using the bamboo mat to help you, roll the maki away from you, pressing gently. Cut into 4 pieces and serve immediately with your favorite condiment, such as sweet pepper relish, tomato chutney or more mushroom ragout.

*Makes 4 cups
(1 L)*

ANTIPASTO MARINARA

One of the most common ways to roast a pepper is to place it on a baking sheet about 3 inches (7.5 cm) under the broiler. Char the skin all over, turning the pepper as it blackens (10 to 15 minutes total). Place in a bowl and cover with plastic wrap (or place in a bag and seal it closed) and let pepper steam for about 15 to 20 minutes. Slip off the skin and remove seeds and core.

For tips on how to choose and clean shellfish, see STEAMED LITTLENECK CLAMS *(recipe, page 97).*

8 oz	shrimp, rinsed	250 g
2 1/2 lbs	mussels, scrubbed	1.25 kg
1/2 cup	white wine	125 mL
8 oz	clams, scrubbed	250 g
2 tbsp	olive oil	25 mL
1	small red onion, finely diced	1
1	small Spanish onion, finely diced	1
2 tbsp	minced garlic	25 mL
2 1/2 lbs	ripe beefsteak tomatoes, seeded and cut into1/2-inch (1 cm) cubes	1.25 kg
2 tbsp	tomato paste	25 mL
1	large roasted red pepper, julienned	1
1	large roasted yellow pepper, julienned	1
1	large roasted green pepper, julienned	1
1 to 2	roasted hot banana peppers, julienned	1 to 2
1/2 cup	large stuffed green olives	125 mL
1/4 cup	capers	50 mL
1 tbsp	anchovy paste	15 mL
2 tbsp	chopped fresh basil	25 mL
	Juice of half lemon	

1. In a large pot of generously salted boiling water, cook shrimp, with shells still on, for about 3 minutes. Drain immediately; cool, peel and slice.

2. In a saucepan with a lid, steam mussels in half of the white wine for 5 minutes or until all have opened. (Discard any that do not open.) Drain, cool and remove meat. Repeat procedure with clams. Set aside.

3. Heat olive oil in a saucepan over medium heat. Add red and Spanish onions and garlic; cook until softened. Add tomatoes; reduce heat to simmer and cook 5 minutes. Add tomato paste; simmer for 30 minutes or until tomatoes are soft. Remove from heat.

4. Add shrimp, mussels, clams, roasted peppers, olives, capers, anchovy paste, basil and lemon juice. Season to taste.

FROM THE KITCHEN OF
ANNE YARYMOWICH

Serves 4 to 6

SMOKED SALMON, APPLE AND HORSERADISH GAUFRETTE

Gaufrettes are wafer-thin, waffled French fries. For the best results, use a mandoline to slice the potatoes. This kitchen tool can slice, julienne and shred vegetables and fruits uniformly, which not only looks great, but also allows for even cooking times. To achieve the waffled cut, slice the potato with a ripple blade at 1/8 inch (2 mm), rotate the potato one-quarter of a turn and then slice again. Continue this back-and-forth rotation.

The gaufrette chips may be made and kept for a week before serving and stored in a tightly closed container.

3	large potatoes, peeled and thinly sliced (into gaufrettes)	3
	Vegetable oil	
	Salt and white pepper to taste	
1 lb	smoked salmon, diced	500 g
2	apples, diced	2
1 tbsp	finely chopped chives	15 mL
1 tbsp	finely chopped dill	15 mL
1	3-inch (7.5 cm) piece horseradish, finely grated	1
1/3 to 1/2 cup	yogurt	75 to 125 mL
	Sprigs fresh dill and/or chives	

1. In a deep-fryer or deep saucepan, heat oil to 350° F (180° C); add potatoes and deep-fry 3 to 4 minutes, turning slices at the halfway point, until golden brown and crisp. Remove from oil and place onto a tray lined with paper towels to drain and cool. Season to taste with salt and pepper.

2. Combine salmon, apples, chives and dill. Stir in horseradish to taste. Fold in just enough yogurt to moisten salmon mixture.

3. Place 1 tsp (5 mL) of the salmon mixture onto each gaufrette. Garnish with chives and/or dill.

FROM THE KITCHEN OF
LILI SULLIVAN

BEET TACO WITH CHARRED AHI TUNA AND PINEAPPLE-VIDALIA ONION SALSA

PREHEAT BARBECUE OR GRILL

*V*idalia onions originate from Vidalia, Georgia and are usually in season in May and June. These large, pale onions have a crisp, mellow flavor that is ideal for eating raw. Two other sweet onions are Walla Walla (from Walla Walla, Washington) and Maui (from Hawaii); both are good substitutes.

Miso *paste, made from fermented soybeans, can be found in health-food and Asian stores. Rice vinegar is sometimes called rice wine vinegar, but is not the same as rice wine (also known as sake).*

The salsa recipe will make more than you need, but it also makes a great condiment for other seafood and grilled chicken and meat.

FROM THE KITCHEN OF
MARK MCEWAN

SALSA

1	pineapple, sliced	1
6 to 8	lemon balm leaves, chopped	6 to 8
1	large Vidalia onion, chopped	1
8	mint leaves, chopped	8
1	green onion, cut diagonally	1
1/2 tsp	sesame oil	2 mL
1/4 tbsp	minced serrano chili	3 mL
1 tbsp	rice vinegar	15 mL
	Juice from 1 lime	
1 tsp	chopped coriander	5 mL
	Salt and pepper to taste	

THAI VINAIGRETTE

1 cup	peanut oil	250 mL
1/2 cup	sesame oil	125 mL
2 tbsp	soya sauce	25 mL
1/2 tsp	minced garlic	2 mL
1/2 tsp	minced jalapeno pepper	2 mL
	Finely grated zest and juice of half orange	
	Juice of half lemon	
1/2 tsp	honey	2 mL
1/2 cup	rice vinegar	125 mL
1/2 tsp	*miso* paste	2 mL
	Salt and pepper to taste	
8	medium-sized pinches sunflower sprouts (about 1 cup [250 mL])	8

BEET TACO

1	large (4- to 5-inch [10 to 12.5 cm]) purple beet, peeled and cut into 8 slices 1/16 inch (1 mm) thick	1
1/4 cup	flour	50 mL
	Canola oil	
	Salt	

TUNA

1 tsp	black peppercorns, crushed	5 mL
1/2 tsp	lemon zest	2 mL
1/2 tsp	orange zest	2 mL
1/2 tbsp	chopped coriander	7 mL
1/2 tbsp	chopped Italian parsley	7 mL
1	green onion, finely chopped	1
2 tbsp	toasted sesame seeds	25 mL
12 oz	ahi tuna, sliced into 8 pieces	375 g

1. Salsa: Sprinkle the pineapple slices with lemon balm. Quickly char over high heat until grill marks appear. When cool enough to handle, chop the pineapple. Blend all the ingredients together and season to taste.

2. Thai vinaigrette: Whisk all the ingredients together except for the sunflower sprouts. Adjust seasoning to taste. Drizzle a little of the vinaigrette onto the sunflower sprouts.

3. Beet taco: In a deep fryer or deep saucepan, heat sufficient canola oil to 350° F (180° C). Dredge beet slices in flour and shake off excess. Using tongs, curl the beet chip in half to form a taco shell. Place in hot oil and deep-fry until crisp. Remove from oil and place on a paper towel to drain. Sprinkle lightly with salt and set aside. Tacos will keep up to 24 hours in a dry place.

Recipe continues next page...

4. Ahi tuna: Mix peppercorns, lemon and orange zest, coriander, parsley, green onion and sesame seeds together. Rub tuna slices into the mixture. Char tuna for 20 seconds on each side until cooked rare.

5. Place sunflower sprouts marinated with vinaigrette into the base of the beet shell. Place tuna on top of sprouts. Add pineapple salsa on top of the tuna; drizzle with more Thai vinaigrette and serve.

SOUPS

SMOKY TOMATO SOUP

Serves 6

Smoked tomatoes give this recipe a flavor reminiscent of smoked bacon or ham. One of Cookstown Greens' unique products, the smoked tomatoes are the result of Ontario specialty grower David Cohlmeyer smoking principe borghese tomatoes with apple wood, cherry wood and maple for about 48 hours.

7	large, ripe field tomatoes	7
1/4 cup	olive oil	50 mL
1	large Spanish onion, chopped	1
2	cloves garlic, minced	2
3	basil leaves, finely chopped	3
2 oz	smoked tomatoes (or sun-dried tomatoes; about 1/2 cup [125 mL])	50 g
8 cups	vegetable stock	2 L
1/2 cup	whipping (35%) cream	125 mL
	Salt and pepper to taste	

1. Roughly chop 6 of the 7 tomatoes. Cut the seventh tomato in half lengthwise and then into half again. Scoop out the seeds and membrane. Cut into small dice and set aside.

2. In a large heavy-bottomed pot, heat oil over medium heat. Add onions and garlic; gently sauté. Add basil, smoked tomatoes, fresh tomatoes and vegetable stock; simmer 5 to 10 minutes.

3. Transfer mixture to a food processor and purée. Force liquid through a sieve. Return strained soup to pot. Add cream and season to taste. (Depending on the variety of tomato and the time of year, a pinch of sugar may be necessary.)

4. Place the reserved diced tomato into each of the bowls. Pour soup on top.

FROM THE KITCHEN OF
JAMIE KENNEDY

COLD YELLOW TOMATO SOUP

Makes 4 cups (1 L)

This soup marries sweet and sour flavors in a very simple recipe. Try using some heritage tomatoes – such as Morden Yellow, Mennonite Heirloom, Yellow Mortgage Lifter or Elbe – for some delicious results. Says organic farmer Alex Nurnberg of Sunnivue Farm in Nairn, Ontario, "People like us grow old varieties so people can learn about them and not forget about them."

"Or their taste," adds grower Don Blakney of Poplar Lane Organic Farm in Alliston, Ontario. "Older people remember what a real tomato tastes like. I'll grow them as long as people will buy them."

FROM THE KITCHEN OF
NORMAND LAPRISE

8	yellow tomatoes, about 4 oz (125 g) each	8
1/2 cup	rice vinegar	125 mL
1/2 cup	water	125 mL
2 tbsp	sugar	25 mL
	Salt and freshly ground pepper	
	Drizzle olive oil (plain, pimiento or tarragon)	

1. Cut tomatoes in half horizontally. Squeeze, remove seeds and reserve the juice. Cut tomato halves into two wedges. Add rice vinegar, water, reserved tomato juice, sugar, salt and pepper. Allow to sit for 1 hour.

2. In a blender or food processor, purée mixture until smooth. Adjust seasoning and pour into bowls. Serve drizzled with olive oil, either plain or infused with pimiento or tarragon.

Organic FACTS

Alex Nurnberg explains that "his" certified-organic farm in Nairn, Ontario is actually held in trust by a non-profit organization. The concept of stewardship land trusts is gradually growing in Canada and allows charitable groups to help preserve land from development or agribusinesses while encouraging sustainable agriculture. The criteria of Sunnivue Farm's land trust states that the property cannot be sold, developed or farmed conventionally, which ensures that Nurnberg and two other growers will always have land to farm organically without having to buy it. Over the years, the farmers have raised and produced organic dairy products, vegetables, chickens, livestock and feed crops and have educated city people about food production. Nurnberg invites children's groups to stay at Sunnivue for a few days "to see what's going on and to get involved in the process and rhythms of the farm."

Serves 4 to 6

COLD ZUCCHINI SOUP WITH LEMON BALM

Lemon balm is a perennial herb native to southern Europe and is a member of the mint family. The upper side of its leaves are downy and, when crushed, emit an aromatic, citrusy scent. Lemon balm is used in salads, poultry and fish dishes, sauces, soups, desserts and even liqueurs (Benedictine and Chartreuse). If lemon balm is unavailable, Chef Labrie suggests chives, basil or coriander.

	Zest of 3 lemons, cut into julienne strips	
2 tbsp	olive oil *or* butter	25 mL
I	large onion, diced	I
I	large leek, washed and chopped	I
5	medium zucchini, chopped	5
8 cups	chicken stock *or* vegetable stock	2 L
3	medium potatoes, chopped	3
7/8 cup	whipping (35%) cream	220 mL
7/8 cup	chopped lemon balm	220 mL
	Juice of I lemon	
	Salt and pepper to taste	

1. Place julienned lemon zest in a pot of cold water. Bring to a boil and refresh in cold water. Repeat procedure. Drain and set aside.

2. In a large saucepan, heat oil over medium heat. Add onion, leek, zucchini and lemon zest; cook until slightly softened. Add stock and potatoes; cook for 40 minutes.

3. In a food processor or blender, purée soup and return to saucepan over medium heat;, add cream. Pour soup into a bowl and refrigerate until cold.

4. Before serving, add lemon balm and lemon juice; season to taste.

FROM THE KITCHEN OF
ALAIN LABRIE

Makes 6 cups
(1.5L)

DANIEL'S CORN CHOWDER WITH HOT SAUCE

*here's nothing like that first cob of fresh, local corn each summer. Juicy and sweet at its best, corn is actually a cereal grain, not a vegetable. Corn has strong mythological meanings to the Mayan, Aztec and Inca cultures — who always farmed organically — and is also referred to as **maize**. Choose cobs that still have their husks tightly on and dampish silk underneath. The stems should be moist and the kernels should emit a milky liquid when gently pierced with your fingernail.*

4 tbsp	butter	60 mL
1 cup	chopped onions	250 mL
1 cup	diced red bell peppers	250 mL
1 cup	diced green peppers	250 mL
1 tbsp	chopped thyme *or* savory *or* tarragon	15 mL
3 cups	vegetable stock	750 mL
5	sweet corn cobs, kernels removed *or* 1 1/2 cups (375 mL) frozen corn	5
2 cups	diced potatoes	500 mL
1 1/2 tsp	salt	7 mL
1/2 tsp	black pepper	2 mL

1. In a heavy saucepan, melt butter over medium heat. Add onions, peppers and herbs; cook until softened. Add stock; bring to a boil. Add corn and potatoes; cover and simmer for 25 to 30 minutes.

2. Add salt and pepper, or to taste. Spoon into bowls and top with HOT SAUCE.

HOT SAUCE

1	Scotch bonnet pepper, finely diced	1
2	jalapeno peppers, finely diced	2
1	onion, finely diced	1
1	red bell pepper, finely diced	1
2	large tomatoes, finely diced	2
2	cloves garlic, minced	2

1. Place all ingredients in a heavy pot. Cover tightly and simmer for 2 hours.

2. In a food processor, purée cooked ingredients; let cool.

FROM THE KITCHEN OF
DANIEL GILBERT

Serves 6

DAIRY-FREE
CREAM OF CELERY SOUP

VEGETABLE STOCK

The addition of millet is what makes this soup creamy without any cream. These small, golden round seeds are a very important staple to Africans since the millet plant is drought resistant and the grain is high in protein. While millet is most commonly used in North America as bird seed, it can make a delicious and nutritious addition to soups, croquettes, muesli and puddings.

Vegetable trimmings such as parsley stems, carrot ends, celery leaves and leek "beards"
(Do not use vegetables from the brassica family, such as broccoli or turnips; their flavor is too strong)

1	**6-inch (15 cm) piece of kombu seaweed**	1
2	**bay leaves (optional)**	2
1	**sprig thyme (optional)**	1
2	**cloves garlic, crushed (optional)**	2
1	**onion, quartered (optional)**	1
10 to 12 cups	**water**	2.5 to 3 L

CELERY SOUP

3 cups	**celery, cut on a 1/2-inch (1 cm) bias**	750 mL
1/4 cup	**millet, washed and drained**	50 mL
6 to 8 cups	**VEGETABLE STOCK (from above)**	1.5 to 2 L
1 tbsp	**extra virgin olive oil**	15 mL
1 cup	**diced onions**	250 mL
2 tsp	**chopped garlic**	10 mL
1/2 cup	**julienned carrots**	125 mL
	Salt to taste	
	Chopped parsley for garnish	

1. Stock: In a saucepan, combine vegetable trimmings, kombu and, if using, optional ingredients. Add water or just enough to cover. Bring to a boil and cook for 15 minutes; strain stock through a sieve. (Stock may be used in stews, soups, sauces and vegetable casseroles.)

FROM THE KITCHEN OF
RON FARMER

2. Soup: In a large pot with a lid, combine celery and millet with 4 1/2 cups (1.125 L) of the vegetable stock. Cover and bring to a boil. Simmer 20 minutes or until both the celery and millet are cooked.

3. In another pot, heat oil over medium heat; add onions and sauté until softened. Add garlic and carrots; cook until soft. Add about 2 cups (500 mL) more stock; bring to a boil. Reduce heat and simmer.

4. Transfer celery-millet mixture to a food processor and purée until very smooth. Pour over sautéed vegetables. Add salt to taste and more stock, if necessary, to achieve desired consistency. Serve garnished with parsley.

Variation

Blend in some chopped herbs such as thyme to give the soup an additional fresh garden taste, or add a little lemon zest or juice.

Makes 6 cups (1.5 L)

CURRIED PUMPKIN AND SQUASH SOUP

The majority of the pumpkins grown in North America are sold for Halloween jack o'lanterns. But the smaller, sweeter sugar pumpkins are often used for pies and soups. Hubbard squash is very large (about 11 lbs [5.5 kg]), ribbed and has an irregular oval shape. Usually greenish in color, the orange flesh is drier than other squash, but very flavorful. The pear-shaped butternut squash has tan skin and orange flesh. Its meat is moist, sweet and smooth tasting.

PREHEAT OVEN TO 375° F (190° C)

12 oz	pumpkin	375 g
12 oz	winter squash (Hubbard or butternut)	375 g
1 tbsp	butter	15 mL
1 cup	chopped onions	250 mL
1/2 cup	chopped celery	125 mL
1	large sweet apple, peeled, cored and chopped	1
1 1/2 tsp	salt	7 mL
1/4 tsp	black pepper	1 mL
2 tsp	curry powder	10 mL
3 cups	chicken stock *or* vegetable stock	750 mL
1	bay leaf	1
1 cup	buttermilk	250 mL
1 tsp	lemon juice	5 mL

1. Bake squash and pumpkin in preheated oven for 30 to 40 minutes or until tender.

2. Meanwhile, in a saucepan over medium heat, melt butter. Add onions, celery, apple, salt and pepper; cover and cook, stirring occasionally, for 5 minutes. Add curry powder, stock and bay leaf; bring to a boil. Reduce heat and simmer for 30 minutes. Discard bay leaf.

3. When baked squash and pumpkin are cool enough to handle, remove seeds (discard or clean and roast as a garnish); peel and cut the flesh into chunks.

4. In a blender or food processor, purée soup mixture with squash and pumpkin. Return to saucepan; add buttermilk and lemon juice. Adjust seasoning to taste. Heat soup through, but do not boil.

FROM THE KITCHEN OF
DINO MAGNATTA

MANITOBA WILD RICE AND WILD MUSHROOM BISQUE

Makes 6 cups (1.5L)

2 tbsp	butter	25 mL
1	small onion, chopped	1
1	stalk celery, chopped	1
3 cups	assorted fresh mushrooms (or rehydrated dried mushrooms with soaking liquid), chopped	750 mL
1 tbsp	minced garlic	15 mL
1	sprig thyme	1
2 tbsp	wild rice pancake flour *or* 1 1/2 tbsp (20 mL) unbleached flour and 1/2 tbsp (7 mL) wild rice flour	25 mL
4 cups	vegetable stock *or* water (include soaking liquid if using dried mushrooms)	1 L
1 1/4 cups	cooked wild rice	300 mL
1	bay leaf	1
1 cup	whipping (35%) cream	250 mL
1 1/2 tsp	salt	7 mL
1/2 tsp	pepper	2 mL
	Sautéed wild rice (optional)	
	Sliced wild mushrooms (optional)	
	Chopped parsley (optional)	

1. In a large skillet, melt butter over medium heat. Add onion, celery, mushrooms, garlic and thyme; sauté until slightly colored. Add flour; cook for 5 minutes. Add stock, cooked wild rice and bay leaf; cook for 25 minutes.

2. In a food processor, purée soup mixture. Stir in cream and season to taste. If desired, garnish with sautéed wild rice, wild mushrooms and parsley.

Many "wild" mushrooms are now farmed, which provides consumers an opportunity to sample a variety of fungi without having to forage through the forest. Cultivated wild mushrooms are grown outdoors on logs or inside on sawdust blocks. The versatility of mushrooms is remarkable: Fruity enokis can enhance a sandwich or salad; meaty portobellos can be stuffed or grilled as an entrée; smoky shiitakes can liven a pasta dish or stir-fry; and delicate oyster mushrooms can accentuate a cream sauce or omelette. When in season, wild mushrooms such as morels, chanterelles, matustakes and porcinis are also readily available.

For directions on how to cook wild rice, see WILD RICE CROQUETTES recipe (page 140).

FROM THE KITCHEN OF
JASON WORTZMAN

LAMB SOUP WITH RED WINE, ROMANO BEANS AND CHÈVRE

Serves 10

This soup is really a meal in itself — and the smell of it simmering in the oven is mouthwatering. If you want to scale down this recipe, you can use a smaller cut of lamb, such as a center leg roast.

Unlike beef, where there are many cuts of meat, lamb offers a more limited selection. A leg of lamb, which comes from the rear leg of the animal, can be bought in a number of ways. The heavier the leg, the older and fattier the lamb. (Generally, to be called a lamb, the animal must be under 1 year old.) Look for pink meat with creamy white fat.

FROM THE KITCHEN OF
CHARLES PART

PREHEAT OVEN TO 375° F (190° C)

1	leg of lamb (about 5 to 6 lbs [2.5 to 3 kg])	1
	Salt and pepper	
2 tbsp	olive oil	25 mL
2 tbsp	butter	25 mL
2	onions, chopped	2
2	carrots, chopped	2
2	parsnips, chopped	2
1	fennel bulb, cored and chopped	1
2	cloves garlic, pressed	2
1/2 cup	red currant jelly	125 mL
1/2 cup	balsamic vinegar	125 mL
3 cups	red wine	750 mL
4 cups	water	1 L
1 lb	plum tomatoes, chopped	500 g
1 cup	Romano beans, soaked overnight and drained	250 mL
1	bay leaf	1
	Thyme and tarragon to taste	
	Freshly grated Parmesan	
	Fresh chèvre (goat cheese), crumbled	
	Zest of 1 orange	

1. Season the lamb with salt and pepper. In a large, heavy ovenproof casserole dish with a lid, heat olive oil over high heat until bubbling. Add lamb and sear on all sides until browned. Place casserole in preheated oven and roast for 45 minutes. Remove from oven and, with a slotted spoon, transfer lamb to a bowl.

2. To the casserole dish, add chopped onions, carrots, parsnips and fennel; cook over medium heat until browned. Add pressed garlic and cook for 2 minutes or until slightly browned.

3. Stir in red currant jelly, balsamic vinegar, wine, water, tomatoes and Romano beans. Add the lamb along with the bay leaf, tarragon and thyme. Cover and simmer in the oven for another hour.

4. Remove casserole from oven. Cut lamb into pieces and return to stock. Adjust seasoning and serve in warm bowls, garnished with Parmesan, crumbled chèvre and orange zest.

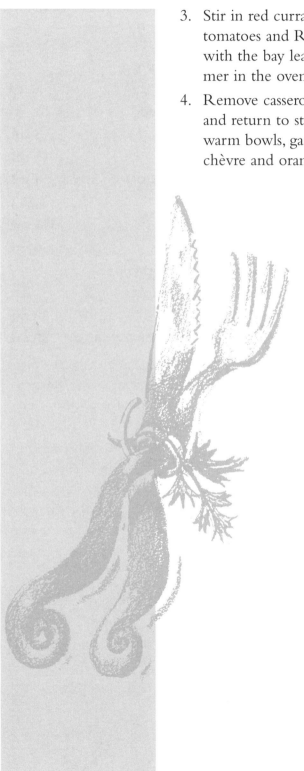

Makes 8 cups (2 L)

SAVORY RED LENTIL SOUP

Lentils were once considered "poor man's food" but that poor person could have done worse. This prehistoric legume is extremely high in protein and is also rich in minerals. Red lentils are often used in Indian dal, croquettes and curries. Here they make a hearty soup delicious. Organically grown lentils, and many other organic legumes, are widely available.

1/4 cup	olive oil	50 mL
1	large onion, chopped	1
1	large carrot, sliced	1
2	cloves garlic, chopped	2
1 tsp	dried thyme	5 mL
1 tbsp	dried marjoram	15 mL
1/4 tsp	curry powder (optional)	1 mL
5 cups	vegetable stock	1.25 L
1 1/2 cups	red lentils	375 mL
1/4 cup	chopped parsley	50 mL
3	medium tomatoes, chopped	3
	Salt and pepper to taste	
1/4 cup	red wine	50 mL
1 cup	grated sharp Cheddar (optional)	250 mL

1. In a large heavy-bottomed pot with a lid, heat oil over medium heat. Add onion, carrot, garlic, thyme, marjoram and, if using, curry; sauté for about 6 minutes or until onion is transparent.

2. Add vegetable stock, red lentils, parsley and tomatoes. Cover and simmer for 1 hour. (Add more stock, if necessary, to achieve desired consistency.)

3. Add red wine just before serving. Garnish with grated sharp Cheddar cheese if desired.

CONDIMENTS

ALLIUM PICKLES

These pickles are guaranteed to make you pucker. They are a great alternative to some of the more common pickles – particularly with the tarragon, which adds a peppery-anise flavor. You can increase the crispness of the pickles by adding wild grape leaves to the jars.

FOUR 2-CUP (500 mL) OR EIGHT 1-CUP (250 mL) STERILIZED JARS AND LIDS

2 lbs	assorted allium such as pearl onions, shallots, wild leeks, green garlic or young onions, trimmed, washed but tips intact up to 3 inches (7.5 cm) long	1 kg
1 tbsp	sea salt	15 mL
1 cup	fresh tarragon sprigs	250 mL
4 to 8	wild grape leaves (optional)	4 to 8
4 cups	vinegar, such as apple cider vinegar	1 L

1. With a knife, cut criss-cross patterns in bottoms of allium vegetables so they will absorb the brine.

2. Fill dry jars, layering allium, salt, tarragon sprigs and, if using, 1 wild grape leaf.

3. In saucepan bring vinegar to a boil; pour into jars. Seal the jars and store at least 2 weeks before serving.

FROM THE KITCHEN OF
PANDORA DE GREEN

CARAMELIZED ONION AND APPLE RELISH

Chef Embrioni serves apple wood-smoked trout with this relish but it's also great with chicken, pork, cheese and crackers.

Certified-organic Alvin Filsinger of Filsinger's Organic Orchards in Ayton, Ontario, grows 25,000 bushels of apples each year. Filsinger offers 35 different varieties including "old fashioneds" – heirloom varieties – such as Red Astrachan and (Chenango) Strawberry. The crisp and juicy, white-fleshed Astrachan would be a good apple for this recipe as it is very tart; the sweeter Strawberry would lend more of a dessert quality to the relish. Other apples good for this recipe are Idared, Northern Spy, Spartan, Cortland and Empire.

1/4 cup	vegetable oil	50 mL
4 oz	butter	125 g
4 cups	diced onions	1 L
4	apples, peeled, cored and cut into 1/2-inch (1 cm) cubes	4
3 tbsp	lemon juice	45 mL
1 tsp	cayenne pepper	5 mL
1/4 cup	honey	50 mL
1 1/2 cup	Riesling (or dry white wine)	375 mL
	Salt and pepper	

1. In a large saucepan, heat oil and butter over medium-high heat. Add onions and cook about 40 minutes or until caramelized.

2. In a bowl toss together apples and lemon juice until well coated. Add to saucepan; increase heat to high and cook for 10 minutes or until apples are brown. Add cayenne pepper and honey; mix thoroughly. Add wine and reduce for 20 minutes. Season with salt and pepper to taste.

FROM THE KITCHEN OF
ELENA EMBRIONI

**Makes 2 cups
(500 mL)**

CHILI-BEET RELISH

Chefs McEwan and Nichols serve this relish with smoked pickerel but it also makes a great addition to sandwiches.

To cook beets: Wash carefully so as not to bruise, tear or cut the raw beets (otherwise they will bleed); trim their tail to about 1 inch (2.5 cm); cover with water and cook for about 30 to 45 minutes, depending on their size. (They will pierce easily when ready.) Beets can also be steamed for about the same length of time as boiling them. Or try roasting beets, which intensifies their sweetness: put in a baking dish or wrap in aluminum foil and bake in a 350° F (180° C) oven until tender, about 1 hour.

PREHEAT BARBECUE OR GRILL

1 to 2 tbsp	olive oil	15 to 25 mL
Pinch	salt and pepper	Pinch
1 tsp	chopped garlic	5 mL
1	jalapeno pepper, chopped	1
1	medium white onion, sliced	1
2	large beets, cooked, peeled and diced into 1/4-inch (5 mm) cubes	2
4 tbsp	olive oil	60 mL
2 tbsp	rice vinegar	25 mL
1 tbsp	chopped coriander	15 mL
	Minced chili pepper to taste	
	Salt and pepper to taste	
1 tsp	chopped ginger root	5 mL
2 tbsp	chopped green onions *or* chives	25 mL

1. In a bowl whisk together 1 to 2 tbsp (15 to 25 mL) olive oil, salt, pepper, garlic and jalapeno. Add onion slices and marinate for 1 hour.

2. Transfer onion slices to barbecue and grill until soft, about 5 minutes. Cool and chop roughly.

3. In a bowl toss together grilled onions and beets. Season with olive oil, rice vinegar, coriander, chili pepper, salt, pepper, ginger and green onions.

FROM THE KITCHEN OF
MARK MCEWAN AND
DALE NICHOLS

Makes 2 cups
(500 mL)

YELLOW DOLL WATERMELON SALSA

Chef Hill serves this salsa with huckleberry-, cranberry- and blueberry-smoked salmon on top of flatbread. It's also a refreshing salsa for chicken.

The sweet Yellow Doll watermelon is the size and shape of a bowling ball and can weigh 3 to 10 lbs (500 g to 5 kg). The rind has dark-green stripes with light green coloring and the flesh is yellow. When choosing a watermelon, look for a heavy melon whose underside (the side that's been resting on the ground) is yellowish, not white. When you knock the melon with your knuckles, you should hear a hollow sound. If you're buying a cut piece, look for melons with dark seeds and deep-colored flesh.

FROM THE KITCHEN OF
JONATHAN HILL

PREHEAT BARBECUE OR GRILL

2 to 4 lbs	**Yellow Doll watermelon (or any other watermelon), cut into 1-inch (2.5 cm) slices**	1 to 2 kg
2	**medium onions, finely diced**	2
1	**small cucumber, diced**	1
1	**medium tomato, diced**	1
1	**small jalapeno pepper, seeded and minced**	1
1/4 cup	**cider vinegar**	50 mL
1/4 cup	**chopped lemon thyme**	50 mL
1/4 cup	**extra virgin olive oil**	50 mL
	Salt and pepper to taste	

1. Grill watermelon slices over extremely high heat for about 90 seconds per side.

2. Remove rind from watermelon pieces and cut into medium to large dice. Place in a large bowl; add onions, cucumber, tomato, jalapeno pepper and cider vinegar. Mix thoroughly. Refrigerate for about 30 minutes. Season with lemon thyme, olive oil, salt and pepper.

Variation

Experiment with other fruits — such as mangoes, pineapples, papayas and cantaloupe — instead of the watermelon.

MAPLE-DIJON VINAIGRETTE

Chef Jamieson serves this vinaigrette with trout, but it also makes a great dressing for salads and vegetables such as asparagus and carrots. This vinaigrette can be kept in the refrigerator for at least 2 weeks.

Technically, Dijon mustard is made in France (mostly in the city Dijon itself) from black or brown mustard seeds, wine or wine vinegar, salt and herbs. Other Dijon-style mustards use similar ingredients, as well as flavorings such as peppercorns, honey or shallots (Dijon mustards cannot). Surprisingly, French law does not specify where the mustard seeds come from, and the majority of the seeds for Dijon mustard come from Canada. A growing number of organic mustards have recently become available.

FROM THE KITCHEN OF
MATTHEW JAMIESON

3 tbsp	Dijon mustard	45 mL
1 cup	olive oil	250 mL
1/2 cup	maple syrup	125 mL
4 tbsp	balsamic vinegar	60 mL
1 tsp	ground ginger	5 mL
1 tsp	salt	5 mL
1 tsp	pepper	5 mL
1 tsp	dried thyme	5 mL
1 tsp	dried oregano	5 mL
	Juice of 1 lemon	

1. In a food processor, blend together the Dijon mustard and olive oil until emulsified. Add remaining ingredients and mix thoroughly. Let sit for an hour.

WILD FRUIT DIPPING SAUCE

This dipping sauce was created to accompany SESAME-SPELT FORTUNE COOKIES (see recipe, page 182) but can also be used with other baked goods, spread on bread or even used to glaze a ham.

Wild ginger has a distinctive gingery smell and taste but is not as spicy or strong as common ginger. Woods with rich soil in eastern and central North America (south to South Carolina) are home to this spring plant, which has a cup-shaped purple-brown flower with 3 pointed lobes.

1/2 cup	white or raw sugar (or 2/3 cup [150 mL] honey or maple syrup)	125 mL
1 cup	water	250 mL
3 lbs	wild pears, apples, crab apples, rosehips, plums or grapes (any combination; if using dried rosehips, reconstitute by soaking in water until soft), washed, quartered, cored and pitted but not peeled	1.5 kg
1	1-inch (2.5 cm) piece ginger root peeled and finely chopped	1
1	whole star anise or 1/2 tsp (2 mL) ground anise	1 2 mL
1/4 tsp	sea salt	1 mL
1	4-inch (10 cm) piece of wild ginger root, scrubbed and grated (optional)	1

1. In a medium saucepan, heat sugar over medium-high heat for 3 minutes or until it starts to caramelize. It should be a rich, dark golden color (especially if using honey or maple syrup).

2. Add water and reduce heat to low. Cook until mixture is smooth. Add fruit, ginger, anise and salt; continue to simmer, covered. Mixture should be bubbling. Cook for 30 minutes or until fruit is very soft. Stir periodically and check to make sure there is still liquid in the pot. A bit of extra water may be added if the mixture is too dry.

3. Purée and strain through a sieve. If desired, add wild ginger to the purée.

FROM THE KITCHEN OF
LAUREN BOYINGTON
& CHRIS
GUSTAFSSON

CRÈME FRAÎCHE

**Makes
1 1/2 cups
(375 mL)**

Crème fraîche is an all-purpose curdled cream that lends a tangy, rich flavor to a number of dishes. It can be used to accompany desserts such as fresh fruit, tarts or chocolate cake and savory dishes such as seafood, or it can be added to sauces, soups, dressings and gratins.

| 1/2 cup | sour cream | 125 mL |
| 1 cup | whipping (35%) cream | 250 mL |

1. Whisk together the sour cream and whipping cream.
2. Pour into a jar or plastic container. Cover and let sit at room temperature for 10 hours or overnight. Refrigerate.

SALADS

Serves 6 to 8

VEGETABLE-QUINOA SALAD

*P*ronounced "keen-wah," quinoa is a highly nutritious ancient grain which originates from the Andes Mountains region. The "mother seed," as the Incas called it, is actually the fruit of a plant, not a cereal grain. Quinoa resembles mustard seed and is covered with saponin, a bitter resin. This natural coating turns foamy when wet, so while quinoa is presoaked and cleaned before it is sold, make sure that the seeds are washed well at home until the water no longer looks soapy.

DRESSING

6 tbsp	olive oil	90 mL
3/4 cup	balsamic vinegar	175 mL
10	cloves garlic, minced	10
2 tsp	salt	10 mL
I tsp	pepper	5 mL

SALAD

3 cups	quinoa, well rinsed and drained	750 mL
6 cups	water	1.5 L
I cup	diced carrots	250 mL
I cup	diced celery	250 mL
2 cups	diced green and red bell peppers	500 mL
1/2 cup	minced parsley	125 mL
I cup	finely sliced green onions	250 mL
3 cups	corn kernels	750 mL

1. In a small bowl, combine oil, balsamic vinegar, garlic, salt and pepper. Whisk together until well blended.

2. In a saucepan with a lid, combine quinoa with water; bring to a boil. Reduce heat, cover and simmer for 12 to 15 minutes until water is absorbed. Let cool.

3. In a large bowl, combine carrots, celery, peppers, parsley, green onions and corn. Add the cooled quinoa and toss gently. Pour dressing over and toss again.

FROM THE KITCHEN OF
JEREMY KING

SALAD OF GREENS, SEEDLINGS AND VEGETABLES WITH SMOKED TOMATO VINAIGRETTE

Serves 4

3	sprigs lemon basil, chopped	3
4 oz	chèvre (goat cheese)	125 g

VINAIGRETTE

2 oz	smoked tomatoes (or sun-dried tomatoes; about 1/2 cup [125 mL]), chopped	50 g
1/4 cup	red wine vinegar	50 mL
1/4 cup	balsamic vinegar	50 mL
	Salt and cracked black pepper to taste	
3/4 cup	olive oil	175 mL

SALAD

2	mixed tomatoes, diced	2
2	mixed peppers, chopped	2
Half	golden nugget squash, roasted and diced	Half
1/4 cup	radish pods	50 mL
1	candy cane beet, cubed and blanched	1
1	gold beet, cubed and blanched	1
8	mixed beans, sliced and blanched	8
4	grape leaves	4
3 oz	greens and seedlings (about 2 cups [500 mL])	75 g

1. Add one-third of the lemon basil to the chèvre. Roll into 12 marble-sized balls and set aside.

2. Vinaigrette: Mix together the remaining lemon basil, smoked tomatoes, red wine vinegar, balsamic vinegar, salt and pepper. Whisk in the olive oil. Set aside.

3. Salad: Gently toss the vegetables together and set aside. Place greens and seedlings on top of the grape leaves; top with vegetables and chèvre. Drizzle with vinaigrette to finish. Serve immediately.

Candy cane beets, also known as chioggia, *reveal pink-and-white concentric rings when cut in half. Both the candy cane beet and the gold beet are varieties that are reputed not to bleed.*

Golden nugget squash is a small, roundish vegetable that resembles a baby pumpkin. Unlike most squash, it grows in a cluster around a central stem, not along a vine.

FROM THE KITCHEN OF
KENNETH PEACE

HOME-SMOKED SALAD OF BLACKENED TOMATO AND ONION ON DRIED VEGETABLE CRISPS

Serves 4 to 6

PREHEAT SMOKER OR BARBECUE

BEECHWOOD PLANK OR SMOKING CHIPS

Half	eggplant, thinly sliced	Half
1	large (4-inch [10 cm]) beet, thinly sliced	1
	Salt	
	All-purpose flour	
2	tomatoes	2
1	golden onion	1
2 tbsp	honey vinegar *or* 2 tbsp (25 mL) cider vinegar and 1 tsp (5 mL) honey)	25 mL
1/4 cup	extra virgin olive oil	50 mL
Half	bunch purple basil, chopped	Half
1	leek, blanched whole	1
2 oz	caraway Cheddar cheese, sliced into rounds	50 g

1. Sprinkle the eggplant and beet slices with salt and flour; place on wire racks. If you have a warm, dry area in your house, allow them to dry there for about 24 hours; if you have a food dehydrator, dry according to the instructions; otherwise, put racks of vegetables in your oven at the very lowest temperature with the door propped open about 4 inches (10 cm). Depending on the temperature of the oven, thickness of slices and the climate, they will take about 6 to 10 hours to dry. Rotate the trays every 2 to 3 hours.

2. Smoke the tomatoes and onion for 1 hour over beechwood. When cooled, slice them thinly and toss with vinegar, olive oil and basil.

3. Cut blanched leek into 1- by 6-inch (2.5 by 15 cm) rectangles; shape into circles and tie with a thin strip of leek. Place on top of the dried beet and eggplant slices.

4. Just before serving, fill the leek mold with the smoked tomato and onion salad; top with a circle of caraway cheese. (The beet slices will bleed if left to sit too long with the salad on top of it.)

Serves 4

ROASTED SHALLOT, GARLIC AND POTATO SALAD

PREHEAT OVEN TO 400° F (200° C)

5	small blue potatoes	5
5	small fingerling potatoes	5
1 tbsp	rock salt	15 mL
3	large shallots	3
2	cloves garlic	2
1 tbsp	olive oil	15 mL
1/2 tsp	toasted mustard seeds	2 mL
1/4 cup	cider vinegar	50 mL
1 tsp	honey	5 mL
1/2 cup	virgin olive oil	125 mL
	Salt and pepper to taste	

Consumers are now blessed with a wide selection of organic potatoes including the less-than-familiar Caribi, Nooksack, Red Lasoda, White Kennebec and Yellow Finn. The blue potatoes called for in this recipe have purply-blue skins and blue flesh and retain their color even after cooking (unlike purple beans). The other potato in this salad, the fingerling variety, is whitish and long. The combination of different colors and flavors work exceptionally well together.

1. Put potatoes and rock salt in a pot and cover with cold water; bring water to a boil. Reduce heat and simmer potatoes until cooked, about 15 to 20 minutes. Drain and let cool. Once the potatoes are cooled, slice into rounds 1/4 inch (5 mm) thick.

2. In a roasting pan, toss shallots and garlic with 1 tbsp (15 mL) olive oil. Bake in preheated oven, stirring occasionally, for 20 minutes or until caramelized and soft. Remove and let cool. Slice roughly.

3. Mix together the mustard seeds, cider vinegar, honey, roasted shallots and garlic. Gradually whisk in the olive oil until emulsified. Season with salt and pepper. Toss gently with potatoes.

FROM THE KITCHEN OF
ROBERT BUCHANAN

SALAD OF ROASTED ROOT VEGETABLES WITH HORSERADISH CREAM

Serves 4

PREHEAT OVEN TO 450° F (230° C)

HORSERADISH CREAM

1/2 cup	grated horseradish	125 mL
1/2 cup	whipping (35%) cream	125 mL
1/2 cup	sour cream	125 mL
	Salt and freshly ground pepper to taste	

VEGETABLES

2	medium carrots, cut into straws*	2
2	medium parsnips, cut into straws*	2
1	small yellow turnip, cut into straws*	1
1	small white turnip, cut into straws*	1
1	medium sweet potato, cut into straws*	1
	Straws should measure 1/4-inch (5 mm) square by 2 inches (5 cm) long	
1	large Spanish onion, peeled and thinly sliced	1
1/4 cup	olive oil	50 mL
	Salt and freshly ground pepper to taste	
	Mesclun mix	

1. Horseradish cream: In a bowl combine horseradish, whipping cream, sour cream, salt and pepper; mix well. Chill.

2. Vegetables: In a large bowl, toss together carrots, parsnips, yellow turnip, white turnip, sweet potato and onion with olive oil, salt and pepper. Place on a baking sheet and roast in preheated oven for 20 minutes or until edges turn light brown. Toss vegetables halfway through roasting time. Remove from the oven and cool.

3. To serve, line a decorative plate with mesclun mix and spoon roasted vegetables on top. Add a dollop of the horseradish cream.

FROM THE KITCHEN OF
WERNER BASSEN

Serves 6

WARM SHIITAKE MUSHROOM SALAD

Shiitakes, which mean "oak mushroom" in Japanese, are traditionally grown on oak logs outdoors. Probably one of the most popular wild mushrooms, shiitakes are meaty and have a strong smoky taste. Certified-organic mushroom grower Bruno Pretto explains that many cultivated mushrooms are heavily sprayed and that the newer chemicals are systemic – so they spread throughout the mushroom. For this reason, whenever possible, buy organically grown mushrooms.

Pine nuts only come from cones in pine trees that are 25 years or older – and most trees do not become a viable source until they are 75 years old. Some varieties of pine nuts are so small that 1,500 are needed to make 1 lb (500 g).

FROM THE KITCHEN OF
BRUNO PRETTO

DRESSING

2 tbsp	toasted pine nuts	25 mL
1 tbsp	finely chopped basil	15 mL
1	clove garlic, chopped	1
2 tbsp	olive oil	25 mL
4 tbsp	vegetable oil	60 mL
2 tbsp	white wine vinegar	25 mL
	Salt and pepper to taste	

SALAD

2 tbsp	olive oil	25 mL
3	large shallots, thinly sliced	3
1 tbsp	finely chopped basil	15 mL
1	clove garlic, chopped	1
8 oz	shiitake mushrooms, stems removed and thinly sliced (about 3 cups [750 mL])	250 g
1/8 cup	toasted pine nuts	25 mL
1 tbsp	fresh lemon juice	15 mL
6 cups	mixed greens (radicchio, arugula and/or endive greens), washed	1.5 L

1. Dressing: In a blender or food processor, blend together all dressing ingredients. Season to taste.

2. Salad: In a frying pan, heat olive oil over medium heat. Add shallots and sauté for about 5 minutes. Add basil, garlic and shiitake mushrooms; fry another 2 minutes. Remove from heat and let cool briefly.

3. Add dressing, toasted pine nuts and lemon juice to mushroom mixture; mix thoroughly. Season to taste.

4. Arrange the mixed greens on individual plates and top with equal portions of the mushroom mixture. Serve immediately.

**Makes 6 cups
(1.5 L)**

TEMPEH-PASTA SALAD

*Tempeh is a highly
nutritious com-
pressed and fermented
soybean cake. Hulled
and cooked soybeans are
innoculated with a healthy
bacterial culture that creates
a Camembert-like rind
over the soybeans.
Tempeh absorbs flavors
very well and is commonly
found in health-food and
Asian stores.*

DRESSING

2 tbsp	olive oil	25 mL
1 tbsp	cider vinegar	15 mL
1/8 tsp	dried oregano	0.5 mL
1 tsp	chopped garlic	5 mL
1 tbsp	tamari	15 mL

SALAD

2 tbsp	olive oil	25 mL
3 tbsp	tamari	45 mL
1 tbsp	cider vinegar	15 mL
2 tsp	chopped garlic	10 mL
1	package (11 oz [340 g]) tempeh, cubed	1
1 cup	uncooked spiral pasta	250 mL
1/4 cup	sliced red onion	50 mL
1/4 cup	sliced celery	50 mL
1/2 cup	julienned red bell pepper	125 mL
1/2 cup	diced green pepper	125 mL
1 tbsp	chopped parsley	15 mL

1. Dressing: In a bowl whisk together all dressing ingredients; chill in refrigerator.

2. Salad: In another bowl, mix together 1 tbsp (15 mL) olive oil, 2 tbsp (25 mL) tamari, vinegar and garlic. Add the tempeh and marinate at least 1 hour.

3. In a skillet heat 1 tbsp (15 mL) of the olive oil and 1 tbsp (15 mL) of the tamari over medium heat. Add marinated tempeh; cook until brown and crispy.

4. In a large pot of boiling salted water, cook the pasta until *al dente*; drain. Toss with the red onion, celery, red and green peppers and parsley. Add the tempeh to pasta-vegetable mixture, pour dressing over and serve.

FROM THE KITCHEN OF
JEREMY KING

SALAD OF CHICKEN AND PEACHES ON SEEDLINGS WITH GRILLED PEPPER DRESSING

Serves 4

1 lb	boneless chicken, cut into 1-inch (2.5 cm) pieces	500 g
1/4 cup	chopped lemon basil	50 mL
1/4 cup	julienned wild leeks	50 mL
1	small red onion, chopped	1
1 tbsp	black peppercorns, crushed	15 mL
1/2 cup	virgin olive oil	125 mL
2	firm peaches, pitted and sliced 1/4 inch (5 mm) thick or 2 cups (500 mL) frozen peach slices	2
3	red peppers, grilled, peeled and seeded	3
2 tbsp	finely minced shallots	25 mL
2 tbsp	balsamic vinegar	25 mL
1 tsp	Dijon mustard	5 mL
3 tbsp	virgin olive oil	45 mL
	Salt and white pepper to taste	
2 oz	mixed seedlings (sunflower, radish or corn)	50 g
	Toasted pine nuts (optional)	

1. In a bowl toss together the chicken, lemon basil, leeks, red onion, peppercorns and olive oil; marinate, covered, in refrigerator for at least 2 hours. Add peach slices and marinate another 30 minutes.

2. Make the dressing: In a food processor, purée red peppers with shallots, balsamic vinegar and mustard. Whisk in olive oil to emulsify; season to taste with salt and pepper. Pour dressing on the bottom of a serving plate; top with seedlings.

3. Sauté chicken and peaches over high heat until chicken is lightly browned and just cooked. Place on top of seedlings and serve immediately. Garnish with pine nuts sprinkled around the salad, if desired.

*B*lack, green and white peppercorns all come from the same plant – their different colors simply represent different stages of ripeness. Green peppercorns are immature berries that are harvested and dried or preserved in vinegar or brine. Black peppercorns are picked when they are half ripened and are turning from green to red; they turn black once they are dried. When the berries are fully ripe, they are picked for white peppercorns. Soaked in water to remove the outer shell, the white peppercorns are the inner seeds of the berries. In terms of flavor, black peppercorns are the most pungent and spicy, the white are milder and the green are fruity. Pink peppercorns come from a totally different plant and have a delicate taste.

FROM THE KITCHEN OF
KENNETH PEACE

Variation

The chicken and peaches can also be grilled. Place them on bamboo skewers (that have been soaked in water for 30 minutes) so they won't fall through the cracks.

SALAD WITH GRILLED QUAIL SPLASHED WITH A STRAWBERRY AND RIESLING VINAIGRETTE

Serves 6

Many cookbooks recommend that you have your butcher debone your quails. And indeed, if you're lucky enough to have a butcher who is willing to do it, get it done – it's a fiddly job. Still, for the majority of people who will end up doing it themselves, here's how: Remove the wings and discard. Next, lay the quail on its breast and cut down the middle of its back. Carefully cut the meat away from the bones or place your fingers between the meat and the skeleton and gently separate. Gradually work your way along the quail so that the meat is left whole. Remove all the bones, leaving the leg bone intact if the recipe calls for it.

FROM THE KITCHEN OF
MARK PICONE

PREHEAT BARBECUE OR GRILL

2 tbsp	extra virgin olive oil	25 mL
	Salt and pepper	
2 tbsp	mixed chopped fresh herbs (such as thyme, oregano, basil, lavender and rosemary)	25 mL
6	quail, deboned	6

VINAIGRETTE

2 tbsp	olive oil	25 mL
2	shallots, finely chopped	2
1 1/2 cups	strawberries, chopped (or any seasonal berries)	375 mL
2 tsp	whole green peppercorns	10 mL
2 tbsp	Late Harvest Riesling (or dry white wine)	25 mL
2 tbsp	balsamic vinegar	25 mL
	Salt and pepper to taste	
1	head red Romaine lettuce, inner leaves and hearts only	1
1 to 2	heads endive, leaves separated	1 to 2
	Chervil to taste	

1. In a bowl whisk together olive oil, salt, pepper and fresh herbs. Add quail, toss to coat and marinate for about 30 minutes. Remove quail, shaking off excess marinade. Grill about 2 minutes per side.

2. Vinaigrette: In a saucepan heat oil over medium heat. Add shallots and sauté until softened. Add strawberries and sauté quickly about 1 minute. (Avoid overcooking berries.) Add peppercorns, wine, balsamic vinegar, salt and pepper to taste. (Chopped berry pieces should still be visible, not mashed.)

3. To serve, arrange salad greens on a plate and add chervil to taste. Place quail off-center of greens. Drizzle with strawberry vinaigrette.

Serves 4

SALAD WITH YELLOWFIN TUNA, TARRAGON, WILD BLUEBERRIES AND PINEAPPLE KETCHUP

If you have a juicer, this recipe will be a snap to make. But even if you don't, the little bit of extra effort is worth the magnificent flavors that Chef Laprise has created here.

If you don't have a juicer, blend or purée 2 yellow peppers and strain through a cheese cloth-lined sieve. For the pineapple "ketchup," blend or purée the pineapple and strain through a fine sieve.

Pimiento oil is made from roasted sweet red peppers.

The vinaigrette and pineapple ketchup can both be made ahead; they will keep well in the refrigerator, covered, for up to 1 week. Let stand at room temperature before serving.

FROM THE KITCHEN OF
NORMAND LAPRISE

VINAIGRETTE

3/8 cup	yellow pepper juice	95 mL
3 tbsp	tarragon oil	45 mL
1/4 cup	blueberries	50 mL
2 tbsp	balsamic vinegar	25 mL

PINEAPPLE KETCHUP

3 to 4 cups	pineapple juice	750 mL to 1 L
3 tbsp	pimiento oil	45 mL
	Salt and freshly ground pepper	
8 oz	Yellowfin tuna	250 g
	Salt and pepper	
1 tsp	olive oil	5 mL
4 oz	mesclun mix, washed and dried (about 4 cups [1 L])	125 g
	Croutons for garnish	

1. Vinaigrette: In a small saucepan, bring pepper juice to a boil. Reduce heat to medium; gently simmer until reduced by two-thirds, about 10 to 15 minutes. Whisk well. In a skillet heat 1 tbsp (15 mL) tarragon oil over high heat; sauté blueberries a few minutes. Deglaze with balsamic vinegar, reduced yellow pepper juice and remaining tarragon oil. Keep warm.

2. Pineapple ketchup: In a stainless steel saucepan, bring pineapple juice to a boil over high heat. Reduce heat to medium and gently simmer until reduced by three-quarters, about 10 minutes. Cool to room temperature. Transfer to food processor and, with motor running, add pimiento oil, salt and pepper until emulsified. Set aside.

3. Season tuna with salt and pepper. In a large nonstick skillet, heat olive oil over high heat. Add tuna and cook about 3 to 4 minutes per side for rare, 5 to 7 minutes for medium. Finely slice tuna and fan onto a plate. Drizzle some of the blueberry vinaigrette on top.

4. In a bowl toss mesclun mix with remaining vinaigrette. Season with salt and pepper and arrange around tuna. Serve with pineapple ketchup and croutons.

Serves 4

SALAD OF LOBSTER FROM MAGDALENE ISLAND

2	lobsters, each 1 1/2 lbs (750 g)	2
	Court bouillon *or* water	
7/8 cup	light (10%) cream, boiled and cooled	220 mL
	Juice of 1 orange	
	Juice and zest of half lemon	
	Tabasco to taste	
	Salt to taste	
1	cantaloupe, *en brunoise** (* see note, lower left)	1
Half	cucumber, *en brunoise*	Half
1	bunch radishes, *en brunoise*	1
7 oz	spinach, washed and sliced (or torn)	210 g
	Toasted sesame seeds to taste	
	Chervil to taste	

1. Cook the lobsters in boiling court bouillon for about 10 minutes. Let them cool 10 minutes. Separate the tail from the body. Take out the stomach, scallop the tails and slice the claws. (Reserve legs for garnishing the plate.)

2. Place lobster corral and the creamy insides into a blender or food processor. Add cream, orange juice, lemon juice, zest and a bit of the court bouillon. Blend to obtain a nice sauce. Add Tabasco, salt, and, if necessary, more court bouillon.

3. In a large bowl, toss together the cantaloupe, cucumber, radishes and spinach. Place equal portions onto the center of 4 plates. Form portions into circles. Top with lobster pieces and cover with sauce. Sprinkle with sesame seeds and chervil. Garnish each plate with small lobster legs.

After much research, the debate over the most humane way to cook a lobster continues. Many well-respected chefs believe that plunging the live lobster head first into rapidly boiling water is the most painless way to end its life. (Although some claim that this also toughens the lobster meat.) Others say that severing the lobster's spinal cord — located where the tail joins the body — with a sharp knife will also kill the lobster immediately. Freezing the lobster for 30 to 60 minutes is another method, as is "drowning" the lobster in cold, fresh water for at least 1 hour.

The term "brunoise" means to cut vegetables in an even, fine dice. A court bouillon is a broth made with water, wine, herbs, carrots, onions and celery and used for poaching or for soups.

FROM THE KITCHEN OF
DOMINIQUE
CREVOISIER

POULTRY

Serves 5

GRILLED TORTILLA SPRING ROLLS WITH FIERY GENOESE BASIL PESTO

This recipe is presented here as Chef Long wrote it for the 1994 Feast of Fields. Genoese basil is traditionally harvested when the plant has about 4 large leaves and a few smaller ones — root and all. This basil has an intense flavor and heady aroma. The best pesto, the Genoese say, is made by hand with a mortar and pestle (hence, pesto).

PREHEAT GRILL OR BROILER

FIERY GENOESE BASIL PESTO

4	bunches Genoese basil leaves, washed and dried	4
1/2 cup	grated Parmesan cheese	125 mL
1/4 cup	garlic cloves	50 mL
3/4 cup	extra virgin olive oil	175 mL
	Juice of 1 lemon	
	Serrano pepper purée to taste	
	Salt to taste	

SPRING ROLLS

1	grilled or pan-seared boneless chicken half – marinated with 1 tsp (5 mL) each minced garlic, crushed peppercorns and chopped thyme, sage, rosemary or marjoram (all, one or some) – finely diced	1
1 cup	julienned red and white cabbage, carrots, onions or any other favorite vegetable	250 mL
1 cup	corn kernels, lightly blanched or roasted	250 mL
1	clove garlic, crushed	1
1 tbsp	toasted sesame seeds	15 mL
1 tbsp	honey	15 mL
1/2 tsp	sesame oil	2 mL
	Juice of 1 lemon or lime	
	Minced serrano or jalapeno pepper to taste	
	Salt and pepper to taste	
10	whole wheat tortillas, 6 inches (15 cm) or larger in diameter	10

FROM THE KITCHEN OF
BRAD LONG

1. Pesto: In a food processor, combine basil, cheese and garlic; purée mixture just until mixed. With motor running, slowly add the olive oil, then lemon juice. When mixture appears to be almost smooth, turn off processor and season with serrano pepper purée and salt to taste. Process mixture for 10 seconds more or until desired consistency is reached.

2. Spring rolls: In a large bowl, combine all the ingredients except the tortillas. Season to taste. Divide mixture equally between tortillas and roll out; warm on a grill or toast under a broiler and allow to rest for 1 minute in a warm (250° F [120° C]) oven. Serve with Fiery Genoese Basil Pesto.

CAJUN CHICKEN "RIBS" WITH GARLIC AND SHALLOTS

Serves 4

Dan Jason of Salt Spring Seeds on Salt Spring Island, B.C., is in charge of a Knives & Forks-funded garlic program for Seeds of Diversity Canada, an organization that preserves varieties at risk. To date, he has more than 50 types of garlic from all over the world and Jason sees "an amazing variety of differences." He grows and maintains the valuable strains and describes them in terms of pungency, texture, size, shape, color and peelability, among other things. Diversity is important to any growing thing, Jason adds, and he appreciates the many features of the collection and hopes others will too.

PREHEAT BARBECUE OR GRILL

2 tsp	salt	10 mL
1 1/2 tsp	ground black pepper	7 mL
1 tsp	ground white pepper	5 mL
1 tsp	cayenne pepper	5 mL
1 1/2 tsp	sweet paprika	7 mL
3 tsp	dried thyme	15 mL
2 tsp	dried basil	10 mL
5	skinless chicken breasts, bone-in, cut into pieces 1/2-inch (1 cm) thick	5
10	cloves garlic, minced	10
14	shallots, finely chopped	14
2 tbsp	olive oil	25 mL

1. In a plastic bag, combine salt, black pepper, white pepper, cayenne, paprika, thyme and basil; shake until well mixed. Add chicken pieces, in batches if necessary, and shake until thoroughly coated.

2. In a bowl mix garlic and shallots with olive oil; coat chicken pieces with mixture.

3. Grill chicken over medium-low heat until cooked, about 15 minutes. (Or bake for about 30 minutes in 350° F [180° C] oven.)

FROM THE KITCHEN OF
DAVID BROWN

Serves 4

BARBECUED CHICKEN BREAST WITH LEMON-GINGER SAUCE

In this recipe, ginger green onion pesto chars the surface of the chicken and infuses it with flavor. This dish, which also works well with chicken legs, is great with steamed rice and your favorite vegetables.

This recipe originally appeared in New World Chinese Cooking, *by Bill Jones and Stephen Wong (Robert Rose, 1998).*

PREHEAT BROILER OR BARBECUE

GINGER GREEN ONION PESTO

I cup	sliced green onions	250 mL
2 tbsp	minced ginger root	25 mL
I cup	vegetable oil	250 mL
1/2 cup	sesame seeds	125 mL
I tsp	salt	5 mL

LEMON-GINGER SAUCE

	Juice and zest of 1 lemon	
2 tbsp	honey	25 mL
I tsp	chili oil	5 mL
I tbsp	minced ginger root	15 mL
I cup	chicken stock	250 mL
2 tbsp	cornstarch, dissolved in a bit of the stock	25 mL
4	boneless chicken breasts	4
	Salt and pepper to taste	

1. Ginger green onion pesto: In a food processor or blender, combine green onions, ginger, oil, sesame seeds and salt. Pulse on and off until mixture achieves a uniform consistency. Transfer to a sealable container and refrigerate.

2. Lemon-ginger sauce: In a small saucepan, combine lemon juice and zest, honey, chili oil, ginger and chicken stock. Mix well and bring to a boil. Add dissolved cornstarch and stir until sauce thickens.

3. Coat chicken with 1/2 cup (125 mL) pesto mixture. (Keep remaining pesto for another use.) Season with salt and pepper. Set aside to marinate for 10 minutes.

4. Grill or broil chicken, skin-side first, until cooked through, about 6 or 7 minutes per side. Slice thinly and top with the lemon-ginger sauce.

FROM THE KITCHEN OF
BILL JONES

Serves 4

SMOKED CHICKEN AND COCONUT RISOTTO

Influenced by his culinary experiences in Asia, Europe and North America, Chef Pryke created this risotto blending exquisite flavors from around the world. Smoked chicken adds a delicate smoky flavor and complements the Arborio and wild rices, coconut milk, lemon balm and dried cherries. Delicatessens and poultry stores often sell smoked chicken at their counters or you can special order them.

For tips on making a great risotto, see WOODLAND RISOTTO (recipe, page 107). For directions on how to cook wild rice, see WILD RICE CROQUETTES (recipe, page 140).

Half	smoked or roasted chicken	Half
3 cups	spring water	750 mL
1	can (14 oz [398 mL]) coconut milk	1
1	small onion, quartered	1
1	clove garlic, crushed	1
1	stalk lemon grass, chopped	1
1	tangerine peel	1
1/4 cup	butter	50 mL
1	medium red onion, chopped	1
1 1/4 cup	Arborio rice	300 mL
1/2 cup	dried cherries	125 mL
1/2 cup	cooked wild rice	125 mL
1/2 cup	fresh peas	125 mL
1/2 cup	chopped lemon balm	125 mL
	Salt and pepper to taste	

1. Remove meat from chicken and set aside. Put stripped carcass into a pot along with water, coconut milk, onion, garlic, lemon grass and tangerine peel; bring to a boil. Reduce heat and simmer for about 1 hour. Strain stock through a sieve. Measure out 5 cups (1.25 L) into a saucepan; keep at a low simmer.

2. In a heavy-bottomed pot, melt butter over medium heat. Add red onion and sauté until transparent. Add Arborio rice and stir to coat. Stir in 1 cup (250 mL) chicken-coconut broth; keep stirring until completely absorbed. Repeat procedure until 3 cups (750 mL) of the broth have been added. Stir in reserved chicken meat and dried cherries.

3. Add another 1 cup (250 mL) broth, stirring until absorbed. Add wild rice and peas. (It should take about 30 to 35 minutes for the risotto to be finished; the Arborio rice should be tender but still firm to the bite.) Stir in lemon balm before serving; season to taste.

FROM THE KITCHEN OF
HERBERT PRYKE

Serves 4

PAPRIKASH CHICKEN

4 tbsp	canola oil	60 mL
8	skinless boneless chicken legs cut into 1-inch (2.5 cm) chunks	8
4 tbsp	butter	60 mL
4	medium onions, diced	4
2 tbsp	minced garlic	25 mL
1/2 cup	sweet paprika	125 mL
8 cups	chicken stock	2 L
2 tsp	lemon juice	10 mL
2 cups	sour cream, at room temperature	500 mL
1 cup	chopped parsley	250 mL
	Salt and black pepper to taste	

1. In a skillet, heat oil over medium–high heat; add chicken and cook until browned all over. Transfer to a dish and set aside.

2. Return skillet to medium heat. Add butter and onions; sauté until transparent. Add garlic and sauté for 2 minutes. Add paprika; cook for 1 minute. Add reserved chicken, chicken stock and lemon juice. Reduce heat and simmer 45 to 60 minutes or until the chicken is tender.

3. Remove from heat. Stir in sour cream and parsley and season to taste.

Paprika means "sweet pepper" in Hungarian and is indeed made from dried and ground sweet peppers. Hungarian paprika is said to be the best quality paprika in the world, and comes in different heat levels. Sometimes the sweet pepper's seeds are used, adding a bit more spice, and sometimes a chili pepper is added, which produces what we know as hot paprika. If you use hot paprika in this dish, start with a smaller amount of spice and then add more to taste later on.

Dumplings, potatoes or rice make a good accompaniment to this dish.

FROM THE KITCHEN OF
MICHAEL SABO

Serves 4

JODHPUR-SPICED CHICKEN WITH GINGERED-PLUM CHUTNEY

As Jodhpur is located in northern India, this recipe is tamer than southern Indian dishes, such as a fiery Madras curry. That's not to say Chef Foote's chicken is mild; you'll find that the ginger-plum chutney balances the chicken nicely.

To dry-roast spices, use a heavy-bottomed or nonstick pan. Shaking the pan constantly, quickly heat the spices over medium-high heat for about 2 minutes. The natural oils in the spices are released by the heat and will give off a spicy aroma.

SPICE MARINADE

Half	bunch thyme, chopped	Half
Half	bunch coriander, chopped	Half
2 tbsp	dry-roasted cumin seed, ground or crushed	25 mL
2 tbsp	dry-roasted fennel seed, ground or crushed	25 mL
2 tbsp	dry roasted black peppercorns, ground or crushed	25 mL
2 tbsp	crushed chilies	25 mL
I tbsp	ground cinnamon	15 mL
	Zest of I orange	
2	cloves garlic, minced	2
	Olive oil *or* vegetable oil *or* yogurt	
I	chicken, cut into pieces	I

GINGERED-PLUM CHUTNEY

2 tsp	vegetable oil	10 mL
Half	medium onion, chopped	Half
I	1/4-inch (5 mm) piece ginger root, minced	I
I tbsp	anise seed	15 mL
1/2 tbsp	black cardamom seeds	7 mL
8	plums, 4 finely chopped, 4 cut into wedges	8
2 tbsp	honey	25 mL
Splash	cider vinegar	Splash
I	bay leaf	I
Quarter	bunch basil, chopped	Quarter
Quarter	bunch mint, chopped	Quarter
Quarter	bunch coriander, chopped	Quarter

FROM THE KITCHEN OF
RENÉE FOOTE

1. Spice marinade: In a large bowl, combine thyme, coriander, cumin, fennel seed, peppercorns, chilies, cinnamon, orange zest and garlic. Stir in enough oil to make a thin paste. Rub mixture all over chicken and marinate for at least 4 hours or overnight.

2. Gingered-plum chutney: In a saucepan heat 2 tsp (10 mL) oil over medium heat. Add onion, ginger, anise and cardamom seeds; cook, stirring, until very aromatic and ginger is softened. Add chopped plums, honey, cider vinegar and bay leaf; cook 20 minutes or until very soft and plum pieces are breaking down. Add plum wedges, basil, mint and coriander. (Sauce is now ready to use or, if you prefer, continue to cook the plum wedges until they are slightly softened, about 10 minutes.)

3. Preheat oven to 400° F (200° C). Season marinated chicken with salt and pepper. Roast chicken for about 20 to 30 minutes or until juices run clear when pricked with a fork (legs will take longer). Serve with gingered-plum chutney and warm flatbread.

Organic FACTS

Many organic farmers are pioneers of their trade and must experiment a great deal. Although Fenwood Farm in Ancaster, Ontario, has raised certified-organic chickens for the past three years, farmer Carol Fennema says she and her husband are still on a "learning curve. There's a lot of trial and error," she admits, such as researching the balance of seed, nutrient and enzyme levels in the feed. Their experiments have paid off — several large grocery chains in Ontario and Quebec are now carrying their chickens.

PHEASANT WITH ROSEMARY-HAZELNUT BISCOTTI, DATE BUTTER AND GRAPE CHUTNEY

Game birds such as quail, pheasant and guinea fowl are gaining popularity in North America as more people look for an alternative to chicken. While there aren't too many certified-organic farmers raising them yet, game birds provide an excellent source of protein, iron and niacin. Pheasant is a lean bird with a delicate, dark-meat flavor. Farm-raised pheasants have a hint of game in their taste, while the wild ones are muskier.

While this recipe may look long, all the components, except for the pheasant, can be prepared up to 1 week in advance.

BISCOTTI

PREHEAT OVEN TO 300° F (150° C)

1/2 cup	vegetable oil	125 mL
6	large eggs	6
1/3 cup	water	75 mL
1 cup	light brown sugar	250 mL
6 cups	all-purpose flour	1.5 L
4 tsp	baking powder	20 mL
2 tsp	salt	10 mL
2 cups	toasted whole hazelnuts	500 mL
3 tbsp	coarsely chopped rosemary	45 mL

GRAPE CHUTNEY

4 cups	Coronation or Concord grapes, seeded (or unseeded grapes)	1 L
3 tbsp	sugar	45 mL
2 tbsp	water	25 mL
2 tbsp	fresh lemon juice	25 mL

DATE BUTTER

1 cup	soft, pitted dates	250 mL
1/4 cup	unsalted butter, softened	50 mL
6	boneless pheasant breast halves, about 6 oz (175 g) each (or 2 whole pheasants, each cut into 4 pieces)	6
	Salt and freshly ground black pepper to taste	
1 tbsp	vegetable oil	15 mL

1. Biscotti: In a bowl, beat together oil, eggs, water and brown sugar until well combined. Sift together flour, baking powder and salt; stir into egg mixture. Add hazelnuts and rosemary. Knead dough briefly until smooth. Shape into four 4- by 5-inch (10 by 12.5 cm) logs and transfer to parchment-lined baking sheets.

Variations

This dish also makes a spectacular appetizer. For the biscotti: After the initial baking, cut biscotti in half lengthwise first, then into 1/2-inch (1 cm) pieces. You should get about 60 square-shaped pieces. Once the pheasant breasts are cooked, slice each one into 10 pieces on the bias. Then spread the biscotti with the softened date butter. Top with 1 slice of the pheasant breast and garnish with the grape chutney. Makes about 60 appetizers.

If pheasant is unavailable, Chef McKinley recommends duck or capon. Cooking times will vary slightly, so check to make sure that the juices run clear when the thickest part of the bird is pricked with a fork.

2. Bake in preheated oven for 45 to 50 minutes until quite firm to the touch. Remove the logs to a rack to cool until warm.

3. With a serrated knife, use a sawing motion, slice into 1/2-inch (1 cm) pieces. You will have approximately 30 pieces. Reduce the oven temperature to 250° F (120° C). Return the biscotti to the baking sheets and bake another 20 to 25 minutes. Transfer to a rack to cool. Store in a tightly covered tin.

4. Grape chutney: In a heavy-bottomed pot, combine grapes (including any skins that may have fallen off the grapes), sugar, water and lemon juice; bring to a boil. Reduce heat to medium and cook, stirring frequently, 20 to 30 minutes or until chutney thickens. Remove from heat and cool; cover and refrigerate.

5. Date butter: In a food processor, purée dates and butter until smooth. Refrigerate, covered, but allow to warm to room temperature before serving.

6. To finish: Preheat oven to 350° F (180° C). Season pheasant breasts liberally. In a large, nonstick frying pan, heat vegetable oil over medium heat. Place pheasant breasts skin-side down in the pan; cook until brown and crispy. Transfer, skin-side up to a baking sheet and bake for 10 to 12 minutes until the juices run clear when the thickest part is pricked with a fork. (If using whole pheasants, bake the legs for about 25 to 30 minutes and the breasts for about 15 to 20 minutes. Check the thickest part of each piece for doneness. The "calf" part of the leg is sinewy so you may not want to serve it.)

7. Serve breasts whole; spread with the date butter and garnish with the grape chutney. Serve biscotti on the side.

Serves 4

GRILLED BROCHETTES OF DUCK MARINATED IN ONION, LIME AND HONEY

Because bees can travel great distances from their hives, organic honey must meet some stringent criteria. To attain OCIA certification the apiary must be at least 6 miles (9.5 km) away from crops in every direction says one organic grower who wanted to get his honey certified but couldn't because of the stipulation. For this reason, he says, most certified honeys tend to come from apiaries in the Rocky Mountains, Alberta and Montana.

Duck is a fattier and bonier bird than most poultry and while there is less flesh, its dark meat is very moist and tasty. Acidic fruit such as oranges, cherries and cranberries are often cooked with duck to complement its rich flavor.

FROM THE KITCHEN OF
PETER OCHITWA

PREHEAT BARBECUE OR GRILL

8 LONG BAMBOO SKEWERS SOAKED IN WATER

	Juice and zest of 3 limes	
Half	large Spanish onion	**Half**
3	cloves garlic	3
1/4 cup	liquid honey	50 mL
1/2 tsp	cumin	2 mL
1/2 tbsp	chili powder	7 mL
1/4 tsp	sea salt	1 mL
1/2 tsp	black pepper	2 mL
Pinch	oregano, rubbed	Pinch
1/4 cup	olive oil	50 mL
1	duck deboned, skinned and removed of excess fat and sinews (or 3 to 4 duck breasts), cut into 1/2-inch (1 cm) cubes	1

1. In a food processor, combine lime juice and zest, onion and garlic. With the motor running, add honey, cumin, chili powder, salt, pepper and oregano. Purée mixture to a smooth consistency; add olive oil.

2. Thread meat onto the skewers and place in a glass dish. Pour marinade over duck. Wrap tightly with plastic wrap and refrigerate for at least 12 hours.

3. Grill over medium-high heat for about 7 minutes or until the meat has reached its desired doneness.

SEAFOOD

CORNCAKES WITH SMOKED WHITEFISH AND BLUEBERRY-MAPLE SAUCE

If you don't have a smoker, you can still smoke the fish with your barbecue. Here's how saucier Lisa Rollo tested this recipe: Preheat one side of a barbecue. Soak 2 cups (500 mL) smoking chips in water for 30 minutes, then drain. Make a trough-like container out of aluminum foil to hold the smoking chips. Place 1 cup (250 mL) dried smoking chips in the foil container and set on the bottom rack over the heated side. When chips start smoking, add some wet chips over top. Turn heat down to low. Place the fish on a rack over a cookie sheet to catch the drippings and put it on the unlit side of the barbecue. If you have more than one level in your barbecue, put it on the upper level. Keep lid closed to keep the smoke inside. Smoke slowly over the lowest temperature until fish is done, about 1 1/2 hours.

FROM THE KITCHEN OF
GARY HOYER

CORNCAKES

2 2/3 cups	flour	650 mL
3/4 cup	cornmeal	175 mL
2 tsp	baking powder	10 mL
2/3 tsp	salt	3 mL
Pinch	pepper	Pinch
Pinch	freshly grated nutmeg	Pinch
3	eggs	3
2 cups	milk	500 mL
2 cups	fresh corn kernels, blanched; half puréed, half left whole	500 mL
2 tbsp	clarified butter	25 mL
1/2 cup	finely chopped chives	125 mL
	Vegetable oil	
	Maple syrup	

SMOKED WHITEFISH

8 cups	water	2 L
1/3 cup	sugar	75 mL
3 tbsp	salt	45 mL
2 tbsp	black peppercorns, cracked	25 mL
4	bay leaves	4
1 tbsp	coriander seeds, cracked	15 mL
1/2 tsp	allspice	2 mL
Quarter	bunch thyme	Quarter
Eighth	bunch savory	Eighth
Eighth	bunch marjoram	Eighth
1	whole whitefish, cleaned and scaled	1
	Maple syrup	

BLUEBERRY-MAPLE SAUCE

1/2 cup	fresh blueberries	125 mL
	Juice of 1/2 lemon	
1 tsp	lemon zest, blanched and finely chopped	5 mL
3 to 4 tbsp	maple syrup	45 to 60 mL
2 tbsp	finely chopped chives	25 mL
1 cup	CRÈME FRAÎCHE (see recipe, page 62)	250 mL
Pinch	salt	Pinch
	Chives	

1. Corncakes: In a bowl stir together the flour, corn-meal, baking powder, salt, pepper and nutmeg. Make a well in the center and blend in eggs and milk, then corn, butter and chives. Let sit for 20 minutes or up to 2 hours.

2. Brush a skillet with oil and heat over high heat. Pour batter to make corncakes about 3 inches (7.5 cm) in diameter. Reduce heat to medium; cook for 2 to 3 minutes per side. When cooked, pat dry and brush with maple syrup. Set aside.

3. Smoked whitefish: In a large pot, combine water, sugar and salt; bring to a boil. Add peppercorns, bay leaves, coriander seeds and allspice; reduce heat and simmer for 10 minutes. Add thyme, savory and marjoram; remove from heat. Let stand until cool. Add whitefish. Transfer to a large bowl and place in refrigerator; allow to cure for 2 days.

4. Preheat smoker or barbecue. Remove fish from curing liquid and pat dry. Smoke slowly for 1 1/2 hours or until done. Brush with maple syrup every 30 minutes or so.

5. Meanwhile, make the blueberry-maple sauce: In a bowl combine ingredients, bruising blueberries with the back of a spoon. Set aside.

6. To serve, top hot corncake with a small piece of smoked fish fillet, a dab of blueberry sauce and a long chive thread.

SOOKE HARBOUR HOUSE CURED HALIBUT

Serves 4 to 6

4 tbsp	sea salt	60 mL
4 tbsp	sugar	60 mL
I	fennel bulb, main stem removed and chopped	I
8	black peppercorns, crushed	8
1 tbsp	mustard seeds	15 mL
6	juniper berries, crushed	6
12	basil leaves, chopped (optional)	12
2	clusters lavender flowers, separated from stems (optional)	2
1 1/2 lbs	halibut fillet, minimum 3/4-inch (1.5 cm) and maximum 2 1/2-inch (6 cm) thick, preferably from the mid-section, skinned (*or* ling cod, greenling *or* cabezon)	750 g
4	Fennel fronds for garnish	4
	Basil leaves *or* flowers for garnish	

1. On the bottom of a stainless steel pan or glass dish, sprinkle half of the salt and sugar; cover with half of the fennel, pepper, mustard seeds, juniper berries, basil and lavender flowers. Place halibut on top and sprinkle evenly with remaining salt and sugar, then with remaining seasonings. Cover loosely with plastic wrap.

2. Place another stainless steel pan or glass dish over prepared halibut and weigh it down with a stack of 10 small plates or some large cans of food (approximately 5 lbs [2.5 kg] or more). Refrigerate from 12 to 16 hours, depending upon the thickness of the fish, until the white-fleshed fish looks translucent or clear and feels firm to the touch. Be careful not to let the halibut cure too long or it will become tough and overly salty. If not eating immediately after curing, remove halibut from brine, wrap in plastic wrap and store in refrigerator.

An essential ingredient of gin, the bittersweet juniper berry is also used in teas, game dishes, marinades, conserves and was once used as a pepper substitute. The resinous blue-black juniper berry only becomes fully ripe after 2 or 3 years on the bush. Look for berries that are free of mould — even dried, they have a high-moisture content — and store in a dry, airtight container.

The halibut can be cured ahead of time and stored in the refrigerator for up to 10 days. A fruit salsa is a good condiment for this dish.

FROM THE KITCHEN OF
DAVID FEYS

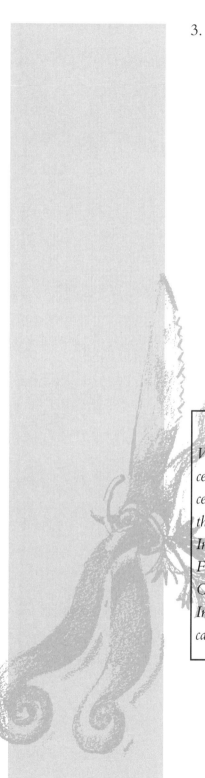

3. Remove halibut from brine; gently scrape off herbs and seasonings. Slice into paper-thin slices vertically through the fillet. Display them attractively on a plate, possibly in a circular pattern. Garnish with fennel fronds and basil if desired.

Organic FACTS

When shopping for organic ingredients, look for an organic-certification logo or designation to ensure that the item is truly certified organic. There are numerous certification bodies around the world, however some familiar ones are the Organic Crop Improvement Association (OCIA), Society of Bio-Dynamic Farming (Demeter), Oregon Tilth, California Certified Organic Farmers (CCOF) and Quality Assurance International (QAI). (For more information on organic-certification bodies, see "Is it really organic?", page 14.)

Serves 4

BOUQUET OF GREENS WRAPPED IN SMOKED SALMON ON A CRISP POTATO PANCAKE

4 oz	mesclun mix	125 g
12	thin slices smoked salmon	12
3	yellow-fleshed potatoes, finely shredded	3
	Vegetable oil	
	Salt and pepper to taste	
1 cup	CRÈME FRAÎCHE (see recipe, page 62)	250 mL

Mesclun mix is a colorful, tasty blend of gourmet salad greens, which varies from season to season and grower to grower. Arugula, baby beet leaves, endive, radicchio, oak leaf lettuce, baby spinach, tatsoi, chervil, mâche, frisée and mustard greens can be found in many mesclun mixes; specialty blends may also include edible flowers such as marigolds, cornflowers and geraniums, pea tendrils, sorrel, dandelion leaves and lamb's quarters. Organic mesclun mix is now found in most large supermarkets and is a popular salad item in restaurants.

1. Wrap a small handful of mesclun mix in each salmon slice to form a small bouquet. Set aside.

2. In a large heavy frying pan, heat a little of the vegetable oil over medium heat. Spread shredded potatoes over bottom of pan to form a thin pancake, about 1/8 inch (3 mm) thick. Cook until golden and crisp, flip over and cook the other side. Remove from pan and drain on paper towels if necessary.

3. Season potato pancake with salt and pepper. Cut into 12 wedges and place a salmon-mesclun bouquet on each wedge. Serve with crème fraîche.

Variation

Add minced fresh herbs to the pancake.

FROM THE KITCHEN OF
KEITH FROGGETT

Serves 4

GRILLED RAINBOW TROUT WITH SHIITAKE CREAM ON POTATO CRISPS

R ainbow trout is the most common trout in North America and originates from the West Coast. Related to salmon, this cold-water species has metallic-blue dorsal skin with varying degrees of pink along its body. The pastel-pink flesh is firm and delicately flavored.

Variation

Instead of frying the potatoes, try baking them. Oil, salt and pepper the potato slices and place on a cookie sheet. Bake at 400° F (200° C) until golden brown, about 30 to 40 minutes. Turn the potatoes over halfway through the baking time.

FROM THE KITCHEN OF
IZABELA KALABIS

PREHEAT BARBECUE OR GRILL

4	rainbow trout fillets	4
4 tbsp	olive oil	60 mL
3	basil leaves, finely chopped	3
	Salt and pepper to taste	
1 tbsp	butter	15 mL
2/3 cup	shiitake mushrooms, cleaned and sliced	150 mL
2	shallots, finely chopped	2
1/4 cup	dry white wine	50 mL
1/4 cup	whipping (35%) cream	50 mL
1 tbsp	finely chopped parsley	15 mL
1 lb	baking potatoes, unpeeled, scrubbed and cut into thick slices	500 g
	Peanut oil	

1. Season trout fillets with olive oil, basil, salt and pepper; place in a dish. Set aside.

2. Shiitake cream: In a saucepan melt butter over medium-high heat. Add mushrooms and season with salt and pepper; increase heat to high and sauté for 2 to 3 minutes. Add shallots and wine; cook, stirring, for 5 minutes. Reduce heat and add cream; cook until heated and a little thickened, about 10 minutes. Add parsley and set aside, keeping warm.

3. In a heavy skillet, heat a sufficient quantity of peanut oil for frying until very hot (350 ° F [180° C]). Drop sliced potatoes into oil and fry about 7 minutes or until lightly browned, turning chips over halfway through cooking. Drain on paper towels. (You can also blanch your potatoes first in 160° F [70° C] oil and then deep-fry them for 3 to 4 minutes right before serving.)

4. Grill trout over medium heat for about 3 minutes on each side. Place a piece of trout on each potato chip and top with 1 tsp (5 mL) of shiitake cream.

Serves 6

SALMON TERRINE

This elegant terrine is time-consuming and expensive to make but the results are memorable. To reduce the cost, eliminate the truffle, which is particularly exorbitant in price. Traditionally, pigs were used to sniff out these underground fungi, but they had a nasty habit of eating what they found; so dogs do most of the truffle hunting today.

The globular black truffle is earthy and imparts its flavor to any food with which it's cooked or stored. For example, if an egg or rice is kept in a glass jar with a truffle, it will taste and smell like the truffle after only a few hours.

White truffles have a much different flavor – somewhat cheesy and garlicky – and are usually eaten raw, grated or shaved into a dish.

PREHEAT OVEN TO 375° F (190° C)

9- BY 5-INCH (2 L) TERRINE DISH LINED WITH PLASTIC WRAP

2 oz	crustless fresh white bread	50 g
5 tbsp	light (10%) cream	75 mL
I	egg white	I
8 oz	salmon fillet	250 g
I tsp	butter	5 mL
I	small onion, sliced	I
I tsp	salt	5 mL
	Freshly ground white pepper	
Pinch	cayenne pepper	Pinch
	Ice cubes (about 2 trays)	
I cup	whipping (35%) cream, whipped	250 mL
I 1/8 lbs	salmon fillet	550 g
	Salt and white pepper	
I oz	truffle, minced	25 g

1. Cut bread into 1/4-inch (5 mm) slices; moisten bread lightly with light cream. Lay sliced bread in a shallow dish. Pour egg white over bread and evenly spoon on remaining cream.

2. Prepare the salmon: Run your fingertips over the fish to check for bones; where necessary, remove with tweezers. Cut the fillet into 1/2-inch (1 cm) cubes. Place salmon on top of bread. Place in refrigerator.

3. In a small saucepan, melt butter over medium heat. Add onion and cook until softened. Season with salt, white pepper and cayenne pepper. Remove from heat and chill, along with bowl of food processor.

FROM THE KITCHEN OF
DAN ATKINSON

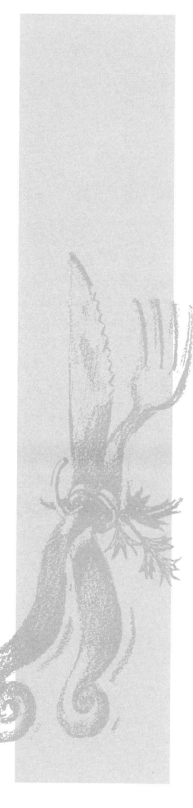

4. Using a very sharp blade (so the meat is minced, not crushed, to release the important proteins that bind the pâté), purée mixture of chilled ingredients in small batches of about 3 to 5 oz (75 to 150 g) each, depending on the size of the processor bowl. The machine must never get hot. If necessary, chill food processor bowl between batches. Mix ingredients to a smooth and uniform consistency.

5. Using a metal scraper, pass the pâté through a metal sieve. This will remove any bones left in the pâté and also improves the quality of forcemeat by removing bits of skin and ligament.

6. Transfer pâté mixture to a bowl and place in a larger bowl filled with ice cubes. Stir with a wooden spoon until the ingredients are thoroughly mixed and mixture takes on a sheen.

7. Adding 1 tbsp (15 mL) at a time, beat whipped cream into chilled pâté mixture. Repeat until all cream is incorporated. The mixture should be light, airy and smooth when finished. Taste and adjust seasoning.

8. Spread about half the pâté mixture onto the bottom of the terrine dish. Cut 12 oz (375 g) of salmon fillet to fit the size of the dish and lay over pâté mixture, skin side up. Season with salt and pepper. Reserve a little pâté mixture; stir truffle into remainder and spread over salmon. Season remaining salmon fillet and place along the center of pâté mixture. Bang down the dish several times and cover its contents with remaining pâté mixture. Bang again, fold over excess plastic wrap and seal.

9. Place the terrine in a larger baking pan filled with boiling water. Cook for 45 minutes, regulating the oven so that the water remains at a gentle simmer.

10. To make the terrine even more lavish, serve with whirls of CRÈME FRAÎCHE (see recipe, 62) and caviar.

Serves 4

RAINBOW TROUT BAKED ON CEDAR WITH MAPLE, MUSTARD AND DILL

This recipe requires a cedar board, between 1/4 and 1/2 inch (5 mm and 1 cm) thick. Some stores that sell barbecue accessories now stock different woods for smoking, or visit a store that carries wood. Soak the board for at least 6 hours prior to using.

Any hardwood can be used here, but don't use softwood – it contains too much resin. Different woods evoke different flavors: cedar and hickory are mild and smoky; cherry wood is sweet and fruity; apple wood is sharp and tangy; maple and alder are mildly sweet; and oak is spicy.

PREHEAT BARBECUE (SEE INSTRUCTIONS BELOW)

CEDAR PLANK

4	rainbow trout fillets (about 4 oz [125 g] each), all fine bones removed	4
2 tbsp	Dijon mustard	25 mL
1/2 cup	maple syrup	125 mL
2 tbsp	chopped dill	25 mL
1 tsp	Worcestershire sauce	5 mL

1. Set up the barbecue, piling 10 coals on 2 sides away from the center of the barbecue. Light the barbecue and allow the coals to burn down. (If you are using a gas barbecue, ignite burner on one side, set to high and let it heat up; place board on unlit side of barbecue and reduce heat to medium-high; continue to cook as for a charcoal fire.) When you can hold your hand 8 inches (20 cm) above the coals for 5 seconds, you have a slow fire and are ready to proceed.

2. Prepare marinade: In a bowl mix together mustard, maple syrup, dill and Worcestershire sauce.

3. Lay trout fillets onto cedar plank. Liberally brush or spoon marinade over trout.

4. Place cedar plank in the center of barbecue (or unlit side of a gas barbecue). Cover with lid or make a tent foil over the barbecue. Let fish to cook for 12 to 15 minutes or until opaque.

5. Serve with a drizzle of remaining warmed marinade.

FROM THE KITCHEN OF
PETER OCHITWA

STEAMED LITTLENECK CLAMS

Serves 4

Make sure that your shellfish is always fresh and that all of your clams are closed. If you have any that are opened, discard them. To clean clams, scrub them well with a stiff brush. Soak them in cold water for about 30 minutes to rinse out any sand that is still on the shellfish (the sand will sink to the bottom). If any of the clams are unopened after cooking, discard them.

Serve this recipe with lots of crusty bread (to sop up all of the broth) or over fresh pasta.

FROM THE KITCHEN OF
MATTHEW JAMIESON

40	littleneck clams, well scrubbed	40
2 cups	julienned leek, celery and/or carrots	500 mL
1 cup	dry white wine	250 mL
1/2 cup	unsalted butter	125 mL
8	cloves garlic, chopped	8
1/2 cup	chopped parsley	125 mL
Pinch	fresh black pepper	Pinch
Splash	Pernod	Splash
4	medium tomatoes, diced	4

1. In a saucepan with a lid, combine all ingredients. Steam for about 5 minutes or until clams open; discard any that remain closed.

*Makes 6
buns*

SOOKE HARBOUR HOUSE HERB-STEAMED BUNS WITH SAVORY SEAFOOD FILLING

BAMBOO OR STAINLESS-STEEL STEAMER

This recipe combines Oriental techniques with local fresh ingredients and an abundance of edible herbs and flowers, says Chef Von Zuben. To fill the kitchen with an appetizing aroma and to give an extra touch of flavor to the buns, Chef Von Zuben makes a herb-scented steaming liquid. He also uses 2 leavening agents — yeast in the dough and baking powder when shaping the dough — which produces light, fluffy buns. If you don't have a vegetable juicer, carrot juice is available through some health-food and specialty stores.

FROM THE KITCHEN OF
FRANK VON ZUBEN

BUNS

3 cups	all-purpose flour	750 mL
1/4 cup	chopped fresh tarragon (or another fresh herb such as chervil, oregano or coriander)	50 mL
2 tsp	white sugar	10 mL
1 tbsp	unrefined corn oil	15 mL
1 1/2 tsp	Ferma yeast (or active dry yeast)	7 mL
1 cup	warm water	250 mL
	Flour for kneading and shaping	
	Unrefined corn oil for brushing	
1/2 tsp	baking powder	2 mL
6	sprigs tarragon tops	6

1. In a large bowl, combine by hand the flour, chopped tarragon and sugar. Make a well in the center; add oil, yeast and water. Mix ingredients with a large wooden spoon until a ball of dough is formed. Place the dough on a floured work surface and knead for 8 minutes or until dough is soft and elastic. (If using an electric mixer [should be heavy-duty type], place flour, chopped tarragon and sugar in mixing bowl; with the dough hook, combine oil, yeast and water; knead for 5 minutes.)

2. Transfer dough to an oiled bowl and brush with corn oil. Cover with a cloth or plastic wrap; allow to triple in bulk (approximately 1 1/2 hours) in a warm place.

3. While dough is rising, make the seafood filling (see facing page).

4. After the dough has doubled, punch it down. Form into a 3-inch (7.5 cm) diameter roll and cut into 6 equal portions.

5. Cover work surface with baking powder and flour; shape dough by hand or roll each portion into a 6-inch (15 cm) round. Make the edges thinner than the center because they will be gathered together.

6. Place 1/3 cup (75 mL) seafood filling into the center; pleat edges to completely enclose filling and pinch tightly to seal.

7. Place each bun (pinched-side up) on a sheet of 5-inch (12.5 cm) square parchment paper (or wax paper). Brush each bun with corn oil and decorate with 1 tarragon sprig. Allow buns to rise until double in volume, about 50 to 60 minutes at room temperature or slowly in the refrigerator.

8. If not steaming immediately, refrigerate buns until ready to cook.

SEAFOOD FILLING

12 oz	salmon fillet, deboned, cut into 1-inch (2.5 cm) chunks	375 g
1	egg white	1
3/4 cup	whipping (35%) cream	175 mL
1/4 cup	Semillon wine (dry white wine)	50 mL
1 tbsp	fennel seeds, bruised	15 mL
1	clove garlic, finely chopped	1
1	shallot, finely diced	1
	Ice cubes (about 2 trays)	
6	large shrimps, shells and heads removed, cut into 1/2-inch (1 cm) chunks (if using East Coast shrimp, devein first)	6
1 1/2 tbsp	finely chopped tarragon	20 mL
1 tsp	salt	5 mL

Recipe continues next page...

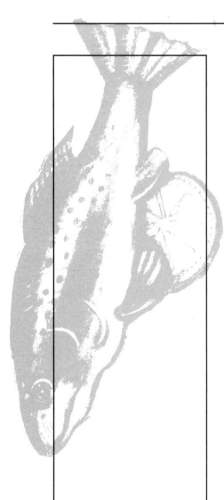

1. Chill salmon, egg white, cream and a food processor bowl.

2. In a small pot, combine white wine and fennel seeds. Bring mixture to a simmer over medium heat and then remove immediately from the heat. Allow to steep.

3. In the pre-chilled food processor bowl, process salmon chunks until smooth. With the motor running, gradually add chilled egg white, garlic, shallot and cream in a slow, steady stream.

4. Transfer mousse to a medium-sized mixing bowl; set bowl inside a larger bowl filled with ice.

5. With a rubber spatula, gently incorporate chopped shrimp, tarragon, salt and strained fennel-seed mixture until a smooth, homogeneous mixture is achieved. Chill until ready to fill buns.

CARROT JUICE GLAZE

5 lbs	carrots (or 3 1/4 cups [800 mL] carrot juice)	2.5 kg
2 tbsp	apple cider vinegar	25 mL
2 tsp	cornstarch	10 mL
1/4 cup	chopped herbs (cilantro, parsley or chives)	50 mL

1. Juice the carrots. (This should yield at least the 3 1/4 cups [800 mL] of carrot juice needed for this recipe.) Set aside 1/4 cup (50 mL) in the refrigerator.

2. In a stainless-steel pot over high heat, reduce 3 cups (750 mL) of the carrot juice to a volume of approximately 2 cups (500 mL), about 20 minutes.

3. Add apple cider vinegar.

4. Dissolve cornstarch in remaining 1/4 cup (50 mL) carrot juice.

5. Beat cornstarch-juice mixture into the simmering liquid and cook for 10 minutes over medium heat. Whisk frequently. Add chopped herbs.

GREEN ONION OIL

| 1/2 cup | sunflower seed oil | 125 mL |
| Half | bunch green onions, green tops only (save the white ends for another use) | Half |

1. Place the oil in a food processor bowl. With the motor running on high, feed the green ends of the onions into the bowl and allow to blend for 2 to 3 minutes.

2. Strain the onion oil through a fine sieve into a 1 cup (250 mL) container.

3. Add 1/2 tbsp (7 mL) of the separated onion pulp to the strained oil.

4. Refrigerate for up to 2 weeks.

TO SERVE

| 1 | handful rosemary, lemon, thyme, oregano, fennel (choose any combination), chopped | 1 |

1. In a wok or large pot of steaming water, add the handful of chopped herbs. Place the buns into a steamer and steam over high heat for 10 minutes.

2. Cut the steamed buns into 4 pieces and arrange them in the center of the plate to show off the filling. Spoon 1/2 cup (125 mL) of the carrot glaze around the bun. Drizzle 1 tbsp (15 mL) of the green onion oil throughout the glaze in a random pattern.

CHARCOAL-GRILLED SPICED SQUID WITH GINGER AND MINT-TOMATO DIP

Also known as calamari, which comes from cala-marius, *the Latin word for "writing," squid emits an edible ink that is used in pasta and rice dishes – and for painting, too!*
Many fish markets will clean the squid upon request, but here's how to prepare it yourself: Separate the tentacles from the body by pulling firmly. Then take out the transparent quill from inside the body and discard. Cut the tenta-cles off just above the eyes and squeeze out the hard beak from the center of the tentacles. Finally, peel off the skin from the body.

MINT-TOMATO DIP

2 tsp	canola oil	10 mL
I	small onion, thinly sliced	I
I tbsp	minced ginger root	15 mL
2	cloves garlic, minced	2
2	large tomatoes, chopped	2
I tbsp	sugar	15 mL
I tbsp	rice vinegar	15 mL
I tbsp	lime juice	15 mL
I tbsp	lemon juice	15 mL
2 tsp	finely chopped green onions	10 mL
2 tsp	finely chopped basil	10 mL
2 tsp	finely chopped mint	10 mL

SPICED SQUID

PREHEAT BARBECUE OR GRILL

12 LONG BAMBOO SKEWERS SOAKED IN WATER

4	whole star anise (or I tsp [5 mL] ground anise)	4
I tsp	white pepper	5 mL
I tsp	cinnamon	5 mL
I tsp	cayenne pepper	5 mL
I tsp	coarse Hungarian paprika	5 mL
I tsp	ground cloves	5 mL
Pinch	salt	Pinch
I 1/2 lbs	squid bodies and tentacles (fresh or frozen)	750 g

FROM THE KITCHEN OF
MICHAEL SABO

1. Mint-tomato dip: In a large nonstick skillet, heat oil over medium heat. Add onion and sauté 4 to 6 minutes or until brown. Stir in ginger and garlic; sauté for another minute. Add tomatoes; reduce heat to low and cook, stirring constantly, until slightly thickened. Add sugar and rice vinegar; cook, stirring constantly for an another 2 minutes. Transfer mixture to a bowl to cool. Stir in lime juice, lemon juice, green onions, basil and mint.

2. Spiced squid: In a blender or spice mill, grind star anise to a powder. Add anise powder to a bowl and mix with white pepper, cinnamon, cayenne, paprika, ground cloves and salt. Rub squid all over with spices.

3. Thread skewers through squid and grill over charcoal fire for 2 minutes on one side, turn over and cook 1 to 2 minutes more. Do not overcook or the squid will be tough.

4. Before serving, remove tentacles from skewers; if desired, slice squid bodies into rings. Serve with mint-tomato dip.

*Makes 6
dumplings*

MUSSELS AND SMOKED-APPLE DUMPLING WITH WILD RICE AND CHANTERELLES

1 lb	mussels, well scrubbed and beards detached	500 g
1 tbsp	canola oil	15 mL
1	yellow bell pepper, diced	1
1/2 cup	diced chanterelle mushrooms	125 mL
2 tbsp	minced ginger root	25 mL
1 cup	cooked wild rice	125 mL
1	apple, smoked or grilled, diced	1
1	egg	1
	Salt and pepper	
	Flour *or* bread crumbs to stiffen	
	Oil for frying	
	Caviar (optional)	
	Pickled daikon radish (optional)	

1. Steam the mussels until the shells open, about 5 minutes. Remove from shells and let cool. When cool, cut each mussel into 2 or 3 pieces, depending on the size.

2. In a skillet heat oil over medium heat. Add yellow pepper, chanterelles and ginger; sauté until softened. Set aside to cool.

3. In a bowl combine mussels, chanterelle mixture, rice, smoked apple, salt and pepper. Stir in egg until well combined. Cool mixture in refrigerator for at least 1 hour.

4. Form mixture into 3-inch (7.5 cm) patties. (If mixture will not form into balls, add about 1 tbsp (15 mL) flour or bread crumbs to stiffen; add more if necessary.) In a nonstick frying pan, heat a bit of oil; add dumplings. Brown dumplings on both sides, taking care when flipping them.

5. Garnish with caviar and pickled daikon radish, if desired.

Mussels are usually found in clusters clinging to rocks, sandbanks or other objects with their "beards" — strong threads that the mussels secrete. Mussels live on both North American coasts however the Pacific coast is often polluted in the summer so mussels are not allowed to be harvested during certain months. Some mussel aquaculture operations raise toxic-free mussels, which are more tender, fatter and paler than the wild ones.

For tips on choosing and cleaning shellfish, see STEAMED LITTLENECK CLAMS *(recipe, page 97). For directions on how to cook wild rice, see* WILD RICE CROQUETTES *(recipe, page 140).*

FROM THE KITCHEN OF
JOHN BABY

Meat

BEEF PENNE WITH SHIITAKE MUSHROOMS IN A MAPLE-LEMON GRASS SAUCE

Although it's related to the cabbage family, bok choy looks more like Swiss chard, with green leaves and fleshy white ribs. It also has a more subtle flavor than cabbage, with a fresh, crisp taste and requires very little cooking. Baby bok choy can be found in specialty grocers and has an even more mellow flavor than the regular variety. If the baby version is unavailable, buy regular bok choy, slice across the ribs, and toss it into the pan with the cooked penne.

1/2 cup	chopped Bermuda onions	125 mL
1/2 cup	chopped yellow onions	125 mL
1/2 cup	chopped green onions	125 mL
1 cup	chopped yellow and/or red bell peppers	250 mL
4 tsp	minced garlic	20 mL
1/4 cup	thinly sliced lemon grass	50 mL
4 tsp	canola oil	20 mL
12	whole shiitake mushrooms, sliced	12
12 oz	beef, sliced	375 g
2 1/2 cups	beef stock	625 mL
4 tsp	*miso* paste	20 mL
1/4 cup	maple syrup	50 mL
4 tsp	gluten-free soya sauce	20 mL
6 cups	cooked whole wheat penne, warm	1.5 L
12 leaves	baby bok choy	12 leaves
	Chopped parsley or coriander	

1. In a wok or large frying pan, heat oil over medium-high heat. Add onions, peppers, garlic and lemon grass; sauté until softened. Add shiitake mushrooms and beef; sear on all sides.

2. Over high heat, deglaze beef-mushroom mixture with beef stock. Add *miso* paste, maple syrup and soya sauce. Reduce the sauce, about 5 minutes.

3. When beef is medium-rare, toss in the warmed penne and serve.

4. Garnish with baby bok choy leaves and chopped parsley.

Variation

Grill the beef whole and then slice thinly. Add it to the pan with the penne.

FROM THE KITCHEN OF
WALTER TELEMANS

Serves 4

WOODLAND RISOTTO

3/4 cup	butter	175 mL
1 lb	raw wild mushrooms (chanterelles, morels, porcini, etc.), washed, trimmed and sliced	500 g
	Salt and pepper to taste	
1	Spanish onion, finely diced	1
2 cups	carnaroli rice (or Arborio rice)	500 mL
2 oz	pancetta (Italian cured bacon), diced	50 g
6 to 7 cups	strong chicken stock, simmering	1.5 to 1.75 L
2 tbsp	chopped parsley, thyme or rosemary	25 mL
2 oz	Parmigiano-Reggiano, grated	50 g

Here are some tips to make a delicious, successful risotto: Use a heavy-bottomed pot with straight sides to keep the cooking even; use unrinsed rice (the starch that coats the rice makes the risotto creamy); add hot broth to the risotto (if cold broth is added, the rice will cool down and it will take longer to cook, which will produce rice with a glue-like texture); be patient — add more liquid only after the liquid in the pot has been absorbed by the rice (the first additions will be absorbed faster than the last few); and, finally, stir often.

Chef Froggett uses carnaroli rice instead of Arborio; he thinks it makes the best-tasting risotto and gives it a wonderful texture. Specialty and Italian stores may carry this pearlish Italian short-grained rice.

Although this recipe calls for a large amount of butter (to add to the rich flavor of the risotto), use less if you prefer, or substitute olive oil.

1. In a large, heavy-bottomed saucepan, melt 1/4 cup (50 mL) of the butter over medium heat. Add mushrooms, salt and pepper; cook 10 minutes or until mushroom liquid has nearly evaporated. Set aside in a bowl.

2. In the same saucepan, melt another 1/4 cup (50 mL) butter; add onion and cook until soft. Add rice and pancetta. Stir until rice is coated with butter. Add enough simmering chicken stock to cover the rice. Stir the rice often, adding more stock as it is absorbed.

3. After about 20 minutes, add sautéed mushrooms and cook another 5 minutes.

4. The rice is ready when it is *al dente*, tender but firm to the bite. Stir in the final 1/4 cup (50 mL) butter, fresh herbs and cheese. Season to taste.

Variation

This risotto can be easily made vegetarian by substituting the chicken stock with vegetable stock and omitting the pancetta or substituting it with sun-dried or smoked tomatoes.

FROM THE KITCHEN OF
KEITH FROGGETT

Serves 4

PORK BURGERS WITH WARM POTATO SALAD WRAPPED IN BIBB LETTUCE

Bibb lettuce is a type of butterhead lettuce — a variety that has soft, buttery leaves that are loose on the head and separate easily from the stem. The leaves are green on the outside (some have a red tinge) with pale green-yellow leaves closer to the lettuce heart. If Bibb lettuce is not available, use another butterhead type such as Boston lettuce.

Variation

Use ground chicken instead of ground pork. Or trying adding a spoonful of Dijon mustard to the dressing before tossing with the potatoes.

FROM THE KITCHEN OF
**MICHAEL
STADTLÄNDER**

BURGERS

3	slices sourdough bread, crusts removed	3
1/3 cup	milk	75 mL
1 lb	ground pork	500 g
1	egg	1
1 tbsp	chopped marjoram	15 mL
1 tbsp	chopped thyme	15 mL
1/4 cup	chopped flat-leaf parsley	50 mL
3	cloves garlic, minced	3
	Salt and pepper	

POTATO SALAD

6	small blue potatoes	6
1/3 cup	hot vegetable stock	75 mL
	Salt and pepper	
1/4 cup	safflower oil	50 mL
1 tbsp	apple cider vinegar	15 mL
1 tbsp	chopped chives	15 mL
1 tbsp	chopped flat-leaf parsley	15 mL
4	Bibb lettuce leaves	4

1. Burgers: In a shallow dish, soak sourdough slices in milk for about 10 minutes. Squeeze out excess milk from the bread; tear into pieces. In a bowl combine with pork, egg, marjoram, thyme, parsley, garlic, salt and pepper. Form mixture into 4 patties. Over medium-high heat, pan-fry or grill the burgers until done, about 10 minutes on each side, depending on their thickness.

2. Potato salad: In a pot of boiling water, cook potatoes until tender but not too soft, about 15 to 20 minutes; drain. Slice the potatoes and transfer to a bowl. Pour vegetable stock over. Add salt and pepper. Whisk together safflower oil and vinegar; pour over potatoes. Add chopped herbs; gently toss the salad, being careful not to break up potatoes. Season to taste.

3. To serve, place a burger on a lettuce leaf; top with warm potato salad and then wrap up.

Serves 4

SPIEDINI OF WILD BOAR WITH SWEET-AND-SOUR GLAZE

Wild boar are popular in Europe and Asia, where they originated and where they still roam freely. According to organic farmer Harro Wehrmann of Huron Game Farm in Ripley, Ontario, wild boar has a "sweet taste like pork with a hint of game flavor but not as strong as deer." The dark-red meat is tender and lean; however, pork may be substituted if wild boar is not available.

PREHEAT BARBECUE OR GRILL

10 LONG BAMBOO SKEWERS SOAKED IN WATER

1	medium onion, chopped	1
1	medium carrot, chopped	1
1	medium celery stalk, chopped	1
4	cloves garlic, minced	4
1/4 cup	olive oil	50 mL
3	bay leaves	3
2	sprigs sage	2
6	juniper berries, crushed	6
3	whole cloves	3
Pinch	nutmeg	Pinch
12	whole black peppercorns	12
1 1/2 cups	red wine	375 mL
3 lbs	wild boar (or pork loin), cut into 1-inch (2.5 cm) cubes	1.5 kg
4 tbsp	red wine vinegar	60 mL
2 tbsp	red currant jelly	25 mL
1 tbsp	honey	15 mL
	Salt and pepper	
12 oz	salt pork (or side bacon), sliced 1/2-inch (1 cm) thick and then into 1-inch (2.5 cm) square pieces	375 g

1. Sauté onion, carrot, celery and garlic for about 10 minutes in olive oil. Add bay leaves, sage, juniper berries, cloves, nutmeg, peppercorns and red wine. Bring to a boil and simmer for 5 minutes. Cool and pour over wild boar. Mix well and refrigerate overnight or up to 2 days.

2. Remove meat and dry. Strain marinade into a saucepan, pressing down well on vegetables to extract most of the liquid. Bring to a boil; cook until reduced by half, about 10 minutes. Add red wine vinegar, red currant jelly and honey. Stir until dissolved; remove from heat.

4. Season meat with salt and pepper. Skewer the wild boar, alternating with pieces of salt pork. Grill for about 15 minutes until done. Brush with sauce frequently.

FROM THE KITCHEN OF
ANDREW
MILNE-ALLAN

Serves 4 or 5

OLD CHEDDAR AND SMOKED BACON GRIDDLE CAKES WITH DARK ALE GRAVY

Cheddar is semi-firm pressed cheese matured anywhere from a few months to about 5 years. While age plays a large part in determining whether the Cheddar has a mild or sharp taste, other factors — such as if it is made from goat's, sheep's or cow's milk — can also make a discernible difference. Cheddars can be crumbly or solid and can be clean tasting, pungent, nutty or mellow.

To roast garlic, cut off just the stem part of the unpeeled clove. Mix with 1 tbsp (15 mL) olive oil and bake, covered, in a 350° F (180° C) oven for about 20 minutes or until soft.

DARK ALE GRAVY

2 cups	chicken stock	500 mL
2 tbsp	unsalted butter	25 mL
I	Vidalia onion, sliced	I
I 1/4 cups	Upper Canada Dark Ale (or any dark ale)	300 mL
2	sprigs thyme	2
3	cloves garlic, unpeeled	3
I tbsp	Dijon mustard	15 mL
	Salt and fresh black pepper	

GRIDDLE CAKES

I	day-old baguette, cut into 1/2-inch (1 cm) cubes (about 5 cups [1.25 L])	I
1/2 cup	flour	125 mL
6	roasted cloves garlic, chopped fine	6
6	slices smoked bacon, medium-diced and cooked	6
2 1/3 cups	grated old Cheddar cheese	575 mL
I 1/4 cups	whipping (35%) cream	300 mL
2	large eggs	2
	Butter or oil for frying	
1/4 cup	grated Parmesan cheese	50 mL

1. Gravy: In a saucepan over medium-high heat, cook stock for about 15 minutes or until reduced by half; set aside.

2. In a sauté pan, melt butter over medium heat. Add onion and cook 15 minutes or until caramelized. Add dark ale and cook 20 minutes or until completely reduced. Add thyme, garlic and reduced stock; bring to a boil. Reduce heat and simmer for 20 minutes. The gravy will reduce by one-third. Remove garlic and thyme. Add Dijon mustard; season with salt and pepper. Set aside, keeping gravy warm.

FROM THE KITCHEN OF
DAVID WATT

3. Griddle cakes: In a large bowl, mix together bread cubes and flour. Add garlic, bacon and grated Cheddar; combine well.

4. In a small bowl, mix cream and eggs until well combined. Pour over bread mixture and fold together until all liquid has been absorbed by the bread.

5. Heat griddle or large frying pan over medium heat; add butter to coat the bottom. Reduce heat to medium-low. Using a 1/3-cup (75 mL) measure, scoop out griddle-cake mixture and form together with your hands. Place onto griddle or pan. Turn after 5 minutes and cook for another 5 minutes. Makes 8 to 10 griddle cakes.

6. To serve, sprinkle griddle cakes with Parmesan and a dollop of gravy, about 1 tbsp (15 mL) per cake. Griddle cakes can be made ahead of time and reheated in oven 5 minutes prior to serving.

Serves 6 to 8

SAVORY STRUDEL OF THAI-CURRIED LAMB AND SWEET POTATO

*W*hen Chef Klugman makes this at his restaurant, he combines cubed lamb, raw onions and seasonings and allows the mixture to marinate overnight in the refrigerator before grinding. This version of his recipe saves some time but if you want a more authentic dish, follow his method. As well, if you don't want to stretch strudel dough, you can substitute phyllo pastry.

A good condiment for this dish is herbed or spiced yogurt (with mustard seed, chives, black pepper, etc.) mixed with mayonnaise. Siracha *sauce is Thai chili hot sauce; both it and Thai curry paste are available in some Asian markets.*

FROM THE KITCHEN OF
CHRIS KLUGMAN

STRUDEL DOUGH

PREHEAT OVEN TO 350° F (180° C)

3/4 cup	warm water	175 mL
3 tbsp	melted butter	45 mL
2 cups	all-purpose flour	500 mL
1/4 tsp	salt	1 mL

LAMB FILLING

3 tbsp	vegetable oil	45 mL
2	red onions, diced	2
2 tsp	chopped garlic	10 mL
1 tsp	chopped ginger root	5 mL
2 tbsp	Thai curry paste	25 mL
1 tbsp	chopped thyme	15 mL
2 lbs	ground lamb	1 kg
1	stalk lemon grass, finely chopped	1
1/4 cup	fish sauce	50 mL
	Salt to taste	
Half	bunch mint leaves, washed	Half
	Siracha sauce *or* hot sauce to taste	
Half	bunch coriander leaves, washed	Half
	Flour for rolling	
3 lbs	cooked sweet potatoes, mashed	1.5 kg
2 tbsp	melted butter	25 mL

1. Strudel dough: In a bowl combine water, butter, flour and salt. Beat well until a smooth dough is formed (this is most easily done in an electric mixer using the paddle attachment). Cover dough and allow to rest in a warm place for at least 20 minutes.

2. Lamb filling: In a medium skillet, heat oil over medium heat. Add onions and cook, stirring, for 5 minutes. Add garlic, ginger, curry paste and thyme; cook 2 to 3 minutes. Remove from heat and allow to cool.

3. Combine onion mixture with lamb, lemon grass, fish sauce, salt, mint leaves, *siracha* sauce and coriander.

4. Assembly: Place a clean tablecloth over a table and sprinkle with flour. Using a floured rolling pin, roll out the dough on the tablecloth to 1/4 inch (5 mm) thick, turning dough over and adding more flour as necessary. Working quickly and carefully, pick up the dough and stretch it (this works well with 2 people) until a thin, translucent sheet is obtained, about 1 square yard (1 square meter). Dot the lamb mixture, then the sweet potato over half of the dough sheet.

5. Roll the strudel by lifting the tablecloth and allowing it to roll towards the area not covered by filling. Continue to lift and roll the strudel until completely rolled up. Transfer to a nonstick baking sheet, cutting the strudel in half if necessary. Brush with melted butter; bake for 25 to 35 minutes until golden brown.

Variation

If you are using phyllo pastry, you will need to put several sheets of pastry together to make it about 1 square yard (1 square meter). Follow the instructions on the phyllo-pastry box on how to work with phyllo pastry.

Serves 4

BLACKENED LEG OF LAMB WITH APRICOT-GINGER MINT SAUCE

The blackening spices for the lamb (salt, garlic, black pepper, white pepper, shallots, cayenne pepper, sweet paprika, thyme and basil) can also be used with many other foods. Among other dishes, Chef Embrioni uses blackening spices to season chicken, corn flapjacks, vegetables, fish, fried green tomatoes and lasagna.

If you want a mint sauce to cool your palate, put only a pinch of chili flakes into the sauce.

PREHEAT BARBECUE OR GRILL

APRICOT-GINGER MINT SAUCE

1/4 cup	olive oil	50 mL
1 tbsp	minced garlic	15 mL
3 oz	ginger, peeled and minced	75 g
1/2 tbsp	chili flakes	7 mL
1 lb	apricots, pitted and quartered (or 2 14-fl oz [398 mL] cans of apricots)	500 g
2 tbsp	soya sauce	25 mL
2 tbsp	honey	25 mL
1	bunch mint, chopped	1

LAMB

1 tsp	salt	5 mL
1 1/2 tsp	minced garlic	7 mL
1 1/2 tsp	black pepper	7 mL
1 tsp	white pepper	5 mL
1 tsp	minced shallots	5 mL
1 tsp	cayenne pepper	5 mL
1 1/2 tsp	sweet paprika	7 mL
1 tsp	dried thyme	5 mL
1 tsp	dried basil	5 mL
1 tsp	caraway seeds	5 mL
1 tsp	fennel seeds	5 mL
1 tsp	mustard seeds	5 mL
1	leg of lamb (5 to 6 lbs [2.5 to 3 kg]), boned and butterflied	1
2 tbsp	olive oil	25 mL

FROM THE KITCHEN OF
ELENA EMBRIONI

1. Sauce: In a skillet heat olive oil over medium heat. Add garlic and ginger; cook for 5 minutes. Add chili flakes; cook for 1 minute. Add apricots; cook for 3 minutes. Reduce heat to low. Add honey and soya sauce; cook mixture for 15 minutes until reduced. Add mint. Remove from heat and allow to cool to room temperature.

2. Lamb: In a large bowl, mix together all herbs and spices. Brush leg of lamb with olive oil; roll lamb in the blackening spices.

3. On the barbecue over high heat, sear each side of the lamb for 5 minutes. Reduce heat to medium-low and cook to desired doneness, about 20 to 30 minutes.

4. Slice the lamb and serve with apricot-ginger mint sauce and flatbread, if desired.

Organic FACTS

The quality of an animal's life has a strong impact on how it will taste, say many farmers. Organic wild boar grower Harro Wehrmann of Huron Game Farm in Ripley, Ontario believes that "you must start with good raw material." Plus a farmer must "match the habitat as close to nature as possible," he emphasizes, "and give them freedom and personal space." By doing this, Wehrmann feels that the livestock will be happy and in good health, two important aspects of an animal's life — and taste.

NORTH-SOUTH CUISINE VENISON BLACK BEAN CHILI

Serves 6 to 8

Jalapenos are fat, thumb-sized green chili peppers with thick smooth skin. When jalapenos are fully ripened and smoked, they are known as chipotles and are a little milder in flavor. What makes peppers hot are the seeds and veins of the chilies, not necessarily the peppers themselves. After cutting chili peppers, be sure to wash your hands well; the peppers contain an irritant that can cause your skin to burn or sting.

1/2 cup	olive oil	125 mL
2	large onions, coarsely chopped	2
8	cloves garlic, minced	8
3	jalapeno peppers, stemmed, seeded and minced	3
3 lbs	venison shoulder (or beef top butt), cut into 1-inch (2.5 cm) cubes	1.5 kg
1 1/2 tsp	salt	7 mL
1/4 cup	canned chipotle chilies (in adobo sauce), minced	50 mL
1/4 cup	New Mexican chili powder	50 mL
2 tbsp	cumin	25 mL
2 tbsp	dried oregano	25 mL
1 lb	fresh plum tomatoes, coarsely chopped *or* 1 can (28 oz [796 mL]) tomatoes, drained	500 g
4 cups	beef stock	1 L
1	bottle (12 oz [355 mL]) Mexican beer	1
8 cups	cooked black beans	2 L
1/2 cup	dried cherries	125 mL
1/2 cup	currants	125 mL
1 cup	sour cream	250 mL
1	bunch green onions, chopped	1

1. In a large heavy-bottomed saucepan, heat 1/4 cup (50 mL) of the olive oil over medium heat. Add onions, garlic and jalapenos. Lower heat and sauté for about 10 to 15 minutes or until onions are tender. Transfer to a bowl and set aside.

2. In the same saucepan over medium-high heat, add remaining olive oil, meat and salt. Cook for about 20 minutes, stirring often and periodically draining off any juice from the meat so that it can brown. (Reserve juice and add to the stock if desired.)

FROM THE KITCHEN OF
LAWRENCE BANGAY

3. Add sautéed onion mixture to saucepan. Stir in chipotle chilies, chili powder, cumin and oregano; cook, stirring often, for 5 minutes. Stir in tomatoes, beef stock and beer; bring to a boil. Reduce heat and simmer, uncovered, for 1 1/2 hours, stirring occasionally.

4. Season to taste. Cook for another 30 minutes or until meat is tender and the chili has reduced to your liking. Stir in black beans, dried cherries and currants; simmer for 5 minutes.

5. Serve with sour cream and green onions.

GRILLED CIDER-GLAZED PORK TENDERLOIN SANDWICH

Chèvre is an unripened cheese, generally made from goat's milk. However, when made with cow's milk, it produces a creamier cheese. While chèvre comes in a variety of shapes, sizes and tastes, its underlying flavor is fresh and tangy — perfect with crackers or fresh fruit, or blended in a cheesecake or pasta dish.

Organic chèvre is not only processed without preservatives, additives or dyes, it is made with organic milk from an animal that has been raised without hormones, growth enhancers or antibiotics, and given only organic grains and feed.

PREHEAT BARBECUE OR GRILL

CIDER GLAZE

2 cups	cider	500 mL
I	bay leaf	I
2	cloves garlic, crushed	5 mL
1/2 tsp	black peppercorns	2 mL
6	whole cloves	6
I	sprig rosemary *or* thyme	I

PORK

I lb	pork tenderloin, trimmed and cut into thin slices	500 g
	Salt and pepper to taste	
I tsp	olive oil	5 mL
I	focaccia (about 10 by 7 inches [25 by 17.5 cm])	I
4 oz	chèvre (goat cheese)	125 g
I cup	baby mustard greens (optional)	250 mL
I	red onion, sliced and grilled (optional)	I

1. Glaze: In a saucepan combine cider with bay leaf, garlic, peppercorns, cloves and rosemary. Bring to a boil; simmer about 30 minutes, reducing glaze until it has the consistency of maple syrup. Strain liquid and set aside.

2. Pork: Season pork slices and lightly coat with olive oil. Place on grill and cook about 5 minutes on each side or to desired doneness.

3. Assembly: Slice focaccia to sandwich size. Just before the pork is finished on the grill, brush with cider glaze. Place pork slices on focaccia and sprinkle with crumbled goat cheese. Before serving, top with mustard greens or red onion, if desired.

VEGETARIAN

Serves 4

CIDER-COOKED SHIITAKE MUSHROOMS WITH GRAINS WRAPPED IN LETTUCE

This recipe, says Chef Gilbert, is totally scalable and adaptable. It can feed 5 or 500 and you can use your favorite grains or substitute some for others.

Here are some tips on cooking the grains used in this recipe, along with their water-to-grain ratio:

Bulgur: *Put grain into a heatproof dish; at a ratio of 2 to 1, pour boiling water over. Cover and let stand for 30 minutes or until water is absorbed. Fluff.*

Wild rice and basmati rice: *See* WILD RICE CROQUETTES *(recipe, page 140) for directions.*

Brown rice: *Long-grain rice 2.5 to 1; short-grain rice 2 to 1. Bring to a boil; simmer, covered, for 35 to 45 minutes.*

Oat groats: *3 to 1; follow method for brown rice but cook for about 1 hour. Add more water after 45 minutes if necessary.*

Wheat berries: *3.5 to 1; soak wheat berries in water overnight; follow method for brown rice but for 50 to 60 minutes.*

FROM THE KITCHEN OF
DANIEL GILBERT

1/4 cup	bulgur	50 mL
1/4 cup	wild rice	50 mL
1/4 cup	basmati rice	50 mL
1/4 cup	brown rice	50 mL
1/4 cup	oat groats	50 mL
1/4 cup	wheat berries	50 mL
1/4 cup	rice vinegar	50 mL
2 tbsp	soya sauce	25 mL
1 cup	apple cider	250 mL
1 cup	sliced shiitake mushrooms	250 mL
1	head Bibb lettuce, leaves separated and left whole	1
	Salt and pepper to taste	

1. Cook each grain separately until tender. (See instructions at left.) Mix cooked grains together with rice vinegar and soya sauce. Cool on a tray so that grains do not become mushy.

2. In a saucepan over low heat, combine cider and mushrooms; cook 10 minutes or until tender. Drain.

3. To assemble, place some of the grain mixture on a lettuce leaf. Add some mushrooms and roll up.

Makes 6 cups (1.5 L)

VEGETABLE-BARLEY RISOTTO

I cup	pearl barley	250 mL
4 1/2 cups	water *or* vegetable stock	1.125 L
I 1/2 tsp	salt	7 mL
2 tbsp	butter	25 mL
Half	small red onion, finely diced	Half
I	small red bell pepper, finely diced	I
I	small zucchini, sliced	I
I cup	chopped oyster mushrooms	250 mL
I tsp	minced garlic	5 mL
3 tbsp	white wine	45 mL
1/2 cup	vegetable stock	125 mL
1/4 cup	grated Parmesan	50 mL
1/3 cup	corn kernels	75 mL
1/3 cup	peas	75 mL
	Salt and pepper to taste	

1. In a large, heavy-bottomed saucepan, cover barley with water. Add salt and bring to a boil; reduce heat and simmer for 20 to 25 minutes until water is absorbed and barley is tender.

2. In a large skillet, melt butter over medium heat. Add onion, red pepper, zucchini and mushrooms; sauté until tender. Stir in garlic; cook for 1 minute. Add wine, stock and barley. Sprinkle in Parmesan; simmer to reduce liquids. Add corn and peas. Season to taste with salt and pepper.

Barley is one of the oldest cultivated grains, dating back more than 10,000 years. It is an extraordinary grain as it will grow under extreme conditions (drought and flood, for instance) and everywhere from the equator to the arctic. It is also a multi-purpose grain, used in everything from beer and bread to casseroles, desserts and soups.

Pearl barley is barley that has been polished several times so the barley's protective layers – including 2 inedible husks and the germ – are stripped away, leaving only the "pearl."

FROM THE KITCHEN OF
LILI SULLIVAN

ROMANO BEANS BRAISED WITH VEGETABLES AND ROASTED RED ONION MARMALADE

Serves 6

PREHEAT OVEN TO 325° F (160° C)

MARMALADE

1 1/2 tbsp	olive oil	20 mL
2	large red onions, thinly sliced	2
1/4 cup	red wine	50 mL
1 tbsp	balsamic vinegar	15 mL
3 tbsp	sugar	45 mL
1/2 tbsp	chopped fresh rosemary (or 1/2 tsp [2 mL] dried)	7 mL
1/4 tsp	salt	1 mL
1/8 tsp	black pepper	0.5 mL

ROMANO BEANS

1/4 cup	olive oil	50 mL
2	cloves garlic, minced	2
1	medium red or white onion, thinly sliced	1
1/2 cup	dry red wine	125 mL
3 cups	chopped tomatoes	750 mL
3 tsp	minced fresh sage (or 1 1/2 tsp [7 mL] dried)	15 mL
1 tsp	salt	5 mL
1/2 tsp	black pepper	2 mL
2 cups	fresh Romano beans, shelled (or 1 cup [250 mL] dried Romano beans, soaked overnight and cooked until just tender)	500 mL
8	mini red potatoes, quartered	8
2 tsp	chopped fresh basil (or 1/2 tsp [2 mL] dried)	10 mL
1/2 tsp	nutmeg	2 mL
1/4 cup	parsley	50 mL

Cooking with wine enhances the flavor of a dish and adds moisture. It can also be used to tenderize meats and poultry dishes. Never use the cooking wines sold in supermarkets as they contain a lot of added salt and could ruin your dish. Use a good quality table wine for the best results.

Popular in Italy, fresh Romano beans are flat-podded green beans. The dried beans are brownish-beige, mottled with reddish-brown; pinto beans can be substituted.

FROM THE KITCHEN OF
WENDY BLACKWOOD

1. Marmalade: In an ovenproof saucepan, heat oil over medium heat. Add onions and cook until translucent. Add red wine, balsamic vinegar and sugar; bring to a boil. Transfer to preheated oven and cook for 45 to 60 minutes, checking every 20 minutes to prevent onions from burning. When onions are tender and most of the liquid has been absorbed, remove from oven. Stir in rosemary, salt and pepper. Set aside.

2. Beans: In a large pot, heat olive oil over medium heat. Add garlic and onions; sauté until translucent. Increase heat, add red wine and cook for 3 to 4 minutes. Add tomatoes, sage, salt, pepper and Romano beans; cook over high heat for 3 to 4 minutes. Reduce heat to low, cover and cook for 30 minutes.

3. Add potatoes, basil and nutmeg. Cook for 20 more minutes. Add more water if too much liquid is being absorbed. Check seasoning and add more sage if desired. Cook for another 15 minutes.

4. Garnish with chopped parsley. Serve with red onion marmalade.

Makes 6 cups
(1.5 L)

VEGETABLE TAGINE

This recipe offers the versatility of using your favorite vegetables and/or what's in season.

To save on cooking time, canned chickpeas have been used in the dish; but if you prefer, use about 1 cup (250 mL) raw chickpeas that have been soaked overnight. Add them in step 1 with the cinnamon and other spices and cook for 1 1/2 hours. (Keep in mind that this will make your hard vegetables softer.)

Serve this vegetable tagine with fluffy couscous.

Half	onion, chopped	Half
I tsp	minced garlic	5 mL
I tsp	minced ginger root	5 mL
1/2 tsp	curry powder	2 mL
1/2 cup	apple juice	125 mL
4 cups	diced hard vegetables (carrots, celery, turnips, parsnips, sweet potatoes, etc.)	I L
Half	stick cinnamon	Half
1/2 tsp	fennel seed	2 mL
2	green cardamom pods	2
2 cups	water	500 mL
I tsp	salt	5 mL
1/2 tsp	pepper	2 mL
2 cups	diced soft vegetables (zucchini, cauliflower, beans, peas, etc.)	500 mL
I	can (19 oz [540 mL]) chickpeas	I

1. In a heavy pot over medium heat, dry sauté the onion, garlic, ginger and curry for 2 minutes. Add half the apple juice and cook until dry. Add hard vegetables; cook for 2 minutes. Add cinnamon, fennel seed, cardamom, water, salt, pepper and remaining apple juice. Bring to a boil, cover and simmer for 30 to 40 minutes

2. Add soft vegetables and chickpeas; simmer for another 20 to 30 minutes. (A thicker sauce can be made by puréeing 1/2 cup [125 mL] of the mixture and adding it back to the tagine.)

FROM THE KITCHEN OF
MARK MOGENSEN

Serves 4

ZUCCHINI BOATS FILLED WITH RATATOUILLE AND HERBS

A good, aged balsamic vinegar is like a fine vintage wine. Some Italians even sip balsamic as an after-dinner drink, which is said to aid digestion. Made with ripe, sweet white grapes, the pressed grape juice is filtered, boiled and left to age and evaporate in barrels. Once it has been concentrated, it is then transferred into smaller barrels of different aromatic woods, and usually matured for a total of at least 5 years (some are aged 100 years).

5	zucchini; 4 cut in half lengthways, 1 diced	5
4 tbsp	olive oil	60 mL
1	medium onion, chopped	1
2 tbsp	minced garlic	25 mL
1	eggplant, diced	1
1	red bell pepper, diced	1
1	green pepper, diced	1
3	medium tomatoes, diced	3
1 tbsp	chopped rosemary	15 mL
1 tbsp	chopped thyme	15 mL
1 tbsp	chopped oregano	15 mL
1 tbsp	chopped basil	15 mL
1 tbsp	chopped parsley	15 mL
2 tbsp	balsamic vinegar	25 mL
	Salt and pepper to taste	
8	sprigs marjoram	8

1. With a vegetable peeler or sharp knife, carefully shave the rounded side of the 4 halved zucchinis so that they will rest flat. With a melon baller, scoop out the flesh. Reserve scooped flesh for the ratatouille.

2. In a large skillet, heat 3 tbsp (45 mL) of the olive oil over medium heat. Add onion and garlic; cook until softened, about 5 minutes. Add eggplant; cook about 10 minutes. Add diced zucchini, scooped zucchini flesh, peppers and tomatoes; cook 5 minutes or until softened. Add herbs, balsamic vinegar, salt and pepper. Reduce heat and simmer for about 15 minutes.

3. Meanwhile, in another skillet, heat remaining 1 tbsp (15 mL) olive oil over medium heat. Add zucchini boats and cook until softened (or grill for about 5 minutes on each side).

4. Spoon the hot ratatouille into the zucchini boats and garnish with marjoram.

FROM THE KITCHEN OF
ANTHONY NUTH &
MARK HOWATT

Serves 4

GRILLED PIZZA WITH CARAMELIZED CORN SALSA AND SWEETENED GREENS

PREHEAT BARBECUE OR GRILL

This pizza is an interesting departure from the traditional cheese-and-tomato-sauce variety. It's quick, simple and it brings together some favorite fresh summer produce. Ready-made pizza doughs are available from some bakeries, delicatessens and supermarkets.

If you are using a small grill, individual-sized pizzas are more manageable. If you don't have a grill or barbecue, the pizza can be baked for 10 to 15 minutes in a 425° F (220° C) oven.

CORN SALSA

2 tbsp	olive oil	25 mL
1 cup	corn kernels	250 mL
1	small onion, halved and sliced lengthwise	1
Half	red bell pepper, finely diced	Half
1	tomato, seeded and diced	1
1	garlic clove, minced	5 mL
1 tbsp	finely chopped Italian parsley	15 mL
1/2 tsp	salt	2 mL
1/4 tsp	pepper	1 mL

SWEETENED GREENS

1 tsp	balsamic vinegar	5 mL
1 tbsp	olive oil	15 mL
1/4 tsp	salt	1 mL
1/8	pepper	0.5 mL
3 cups	mesclun mix	750 mL

14 oz	pizza dough	425 g
	Vegetable oil	

1. Salsa: In a saucepan heat oil over medium heat. Add corn and onion. Reduce heat and cook, stirring frequently, 15 minutes or until corn and onion are well browned (caramelized). Remove from heat and, when cool, toss in red pepper, tomato, garlic, parsley, salt and pepper. Set aside.

2. Greens: In a bowl whisk together vinegar and oil. Season to taste with salt and pepper. Toss vinaigrette with the mesclun mix.

FROM THE KITCHEN OF
DAVID CATENARO

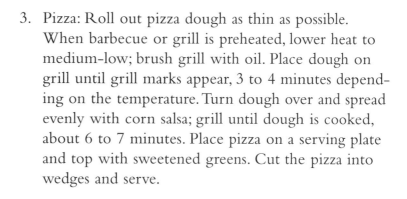

3. Pizza: Roll out pizza dough as thin as possible. When barbecue or grill is preheated, lower heat to medium-low; brush grill with oil. Place dough on grill until grill marks appear, 3 to 4 minutes depending on the temperature. Turn dough over and spread evenly with corn salsa; grill until dough is cooked, about 6 to 7 minutes. Place pizza on a serving plate and top with sweetened greens. Cut the pizza into wedges and serve.

Organic FACTS

In the early 1990s, when Don Blakney and John Camilleri of Poplar Lane Organic Farm in Alliston, Ontario first started selling their organic produce at Toronto's St. Lawrence Market North, their customers were mostly people looking for organic food, Blakney recalls. Now, however, "it's 50-50. New customers come on line because our food looks good and tastes good," and being organic is just an unexpected bonus. One of the reasons that Poplar Lane's produce is so enticing to market goers is because of its incredible freshness – produce is harvested on Thursday, refrigerated and ready for sale Saturday at five a.m.

PECAN BURGER AND THREE-ONION MARMALADE

Pecan trees are native to the United States and most pecans are cultivated in several southern states, from New Mexico eastward to Georgia. A productive tree – some of which have been known to live hundreds of years – can yield about 400 lbs (180 kg) of pecans each season. Most harvesting is done mechanically, with machines that shake the trees, sweep the nuts and then vacuum them up. Pecans have a sweet, rich taste and, once shelled, should be kept refrigerated.

ONION MARMALADE

1 tbsp	olive oil	15 mL
1 cup	Spanish onions, sliced lengthwise	250 mL
1 cup	red onions, sliced lengthwise	250 mL
1 tbsp	lime juice	15 mL
4 tbsp	lemon juice	60 mL
3/4 cup	orange juice	175 mL
1 tbsp	citrus zest	15 mL
2 tbsp	honey	25 mL
2 tbsp	brown sugar	25 mL
1	jalapeno, seeded and diced	1
1 tsp	chopped thyme	5 mL
1	bay leaf	1
1/4 cup	water	50 mL
1 cup	chopped green onions	250 mL

BURGER

1 cup	ground pecans	250 mL
1/2 cup	wheat germ	125 mL
1/2 cup	minced onions	125 mL
1/2 cup	rolled oats, cooked	125 mL
1 cup	minced carrots	250 mL
1 tsp	minced garlic	5 mL
1 1/2 tbsp	sesame oil	20 mL
1	egg	1
3 tbsp	whole wheat flour	45 mL
3 tbsp	chopped herbs (chives, oregano, basil, etc.)	45 mL
6 to 8	buns	6 to 8

FROM THE KITCHEN OF
ANTONIO DE LUCA

1. Marmalade: In a skillet heat olive oil over medium heat. Add Spanish and red onions; cook for about 10 minutes or until golden. Add citrus juices and zest, honey, sugar, jalapeno, thyme, bay leaf and water. Reduce heat and cook 10 to 15 minutes or until almost dry. Add green onions and set aside.

2. Burgers: In a bowl combine pecans, wheat germ, onions, oats, carrots, garlic, sesame oil, egg, whole wheat flour and herbs; mix well. Form into round patties about 3 to 4 inches (7.5 to 10 cm) across, adding more flour as necessary to stiffen the mix.

3. In a nonstick pan, sauté each patty 15 minutes per side or until golden brown. Serve on buns accompanied by onion marmalade.

VALENCIA TOMATO, ONION, CORN AND CHILI PEPPER PIE

Serves 4 to 6

This recipe makes a delicious light dinner or summer brunch. The refreshing flavors of sweet Bermuda onion and fresh corn are accented by the burst of tomato and the tang of chèvre. The minced herbs in the crust gives each bite an additional taste of the garden.

PREHEAT OVEN TO 375° F (190° C)
9-INCH (22.5 CM) PIE PAN

PASTRY

I cup	whole wheat flour	250 mL
1/2 tsp	salt	2 mL
I tsp	minced coriander	5 mL
1/2 tsp	minced chilies	2 mL
2 tsp	minced chives	10 mL
1/2 cup	shortening	125 mL
	Ice water	

FILLING

I	medium Bermuda onion, chopped	I
I to 2	chili peppers, minced (to taste)	I to 2
2	cobs corn, cut off the cob	2
I	Valencia tomato, sliced	I
	Salt and pepper	
I tbsp	minced coriander (or your favorite herb)	15 mL
I cup	grated Monterey Jack cheese	250 mL
I tbsp	chèvre (goat cheese)	15 mL
4	eggs	4
I cup	light (10%) cream	250 mL
1/2 cup	milk	125 mL
	Salt and pepper	

1. Pastry: In a bowl combine flour, salt, coriander, chilies and chives. With a pastry cutter or 2 knives, cut in shortening until it is the size of small peas. Add enough ice water to moisten, about 1/4 cup (50 mL). Roll out pastry to fit pie pan. Flute edges.

FROM THE KITCHEN OF
MELVA BUELL

2. Filling: In a bowl toss together onion, chili pepper and corn. Place mixture in the unbaked pie shell. Arrange tomato slices over vegetables. Season with salt, pepper and coriander. Top with Monterey Jack cheese and chèvre.

3. To finish pie: In a bowl, beat together the eggs, cream, milk, salt and pepper. Pour mixture over the vegetable and cheese filling in the pie shell. Bake until golden brown and set, about 45 to 60 minutes.

Organic FACTS

To control pests without toxic pesticides, some organic farmers use biological controls, which involves using other insects (called predator insects) to eat the pest insects. For more than 16 years, Applied Bio-nomics Ltd. in Sidney, B.C. has been researching, developing and marketing predators for greenhouses, field crops, orchards, conservatories, etc. across North America. In its own greenhouses, the company first has to breed the pests before the predators are introduced. Once they are released, they eat the pests, multiply and are then collected for shipping. Co-owner Don Elliot explains that for a greenhouse whitefly or sweet potato whitefly problem, which can plague tomatoes, cucumbers and peppers, either the whitefly parasite or the whitefly predator beetle can be used. Field mite predators, on the other hand, can be used to control the two-spotted spider mite, which can attack apple orchards, strawberries and raspberries.

PROVENÇAL HERB CRÊPES FILLED WITH SHIITAKE MUSHROOMS AND RICOTTA CHEESE

Makes 12 crêpes

Ricotta is an unripened cheese that was originally a byproduct of the whey left over from making mozzarella cheese. This fresh, high-moisture cheese is mildly sweet and creamy and is often used in both savory dishes such as lasagna and in desserts such as cheesecake.

CRÊPES

1/4 cup	chopped parsley	50 mL
2 tbsp	chopped basil	25 mL
2 tbsp	chopped dill	25 mL
2 tbsp	vegetable oil	25 mL
3/4 cup	all-purpose flour	175 mL
3	eggs, lightly beaten	3
1 cup	milk	250 mL
2 tbsp	butter	25 mL

FILLING

2 tbsp	butter	25 mL
1 1/2 tbsp	vegetable oil	20 mL
1 1/2 tbsp	garlic, minced	20 mL
3	green onions, finely chopped	3
10 oz	shiitake mushrooms, stems trimmed and sliced into thin strips	300 g
1/2 tbsp	lemon juice	7 mL
1	container (1 lb [475 g]) ricotta cheese	1
1/3 cup	chopped parsley	75 mL
1 tsp	salt	5 mL
1/4 tsp	pepper	1 mL

1. Crêpes: In a bowl, blend herbs and oil together; set aside. Sift flour into another bowl; slowly whisk in eggs, herb-oil mixture and milk; whisk until a smooth batter forms.

2. In a nonstick skillet, melt butter over medium heat. Pour in 1/4 cup (50 mL) batter, swirling pan to spread out evenly. When batter bubbles all over or is slightly brown underneath, carefully flip crêpe and cook other side. Repeat procedure with remaining batter. (You should have enough for 12 crêpes.) Stack crêpes and set aside to cool.

FROM THE KITCHEN OF
DINO MAGNATTA

3. Filling: In a skillet, heat butter and oil over medium heat. Add garlic, green onions, shiitake mushrooms and lemon juice; cook gently until tender and lightly browned. Drain and set aside to cool.

4. In a bowl toss ricotta cheese with cooled mushroom mixture and chopped parsley. Add salt and pepper to taste.

5. To finish: Place 2 to 3 tbsp (25 to 45 mL) of filling in each crêpe; roll, tucking in edges.

GNOCCHI PARISIENNE

Serves 6

If you don't have a pastry bag to pipe the gnocchi, you can make it by hand: On a lightly floured board, form mixture into a roll 1/2 inch (1 cm) thick; cut roll into 1-inch (2.5 cm) lengths.

You can add an extra touch by putting your thumbprint or a fork impression into the gnocchi to give it some texture, as well as a place to collect the sauce.

1 cup	milk	250 mL
1 cup	water	250 mL
8 oz	butter	250 g
1/2 tbsp	salt	7 mL
2 1/2 cups	all-purpose flour	625 mL
9	eggs	9
1 lb	spinach, blanched and puréed or 2 bags 10 oz [300 g] washed spinach	500 g
	Melted butter and Parmesan cheese or your favorite pasta sauce	

1. Bring a large pot of salted water to a boil.

2. In a saucepan combine milk, water, butter and salt. Bring to a boil. Add flour all at once and stir well with a wooden spoon. Remove saucepan from heat and beat in eggs, one at a time. Fold in spinach.

3. Fill pastry bag with gnocchi mixture and pipe into boiling water, cutting off 3/4-inch (1.75 cm) pieces of dough with knife.

4. Cook gnocchi until they float, about 3 to 4 minutes. Remove with a slotted spoon and refresh in ice water. Drain.

5. Toss gnocchi with melted butter and Parmesan. Bake for 10 minutes in a 350° F (180° C) oven. (Or just cover with your favorite sauce and serve.)

FROM THE KITCHEN OF
WERNER BASSEN

Serves 4

SPAGHETTI D'ESTATE

1 lb	spaghetti	500 g
2 tbsp	olive oil	25 mL
1 tbsp	minced garlic	15 mL
1/2 tsp	minced chili pepper	2 mL
2 cups	tomato concassé	500 mL
1/2 cup	sun-dried tomatoes	125 mL
1/4 cup	Kalamata olives, pitted	50 mL
1/4 cup	basil, cut into very fine strips	50 mL
1 cup	white wine	250 mL
2 tbsp	butter	25 mL

Grated Parmesan cheese to taste

1. In a large pot of boiling salted water, cook pasta until *al dente*. Drain, reserving some of the pasta water.

2. In a skillet heat olive oil over medium heat. Add garlic and chili pepper; cook for about 4 minutes or until softened. Add tomato concassé, sun-dried tomatoes, olives and basil; sauté for 7 minutes or until cooked. Add white wine and some cooking water from the pasta until brothy. Mix in butter. Toss pasta in; add Parmesan cheese to taste.

Tomato concassé is simply peeled, seeded and diced tomato. To peel a tomato, cut a shallow cross in the bottom of the tomato and drop it in rapidly boiling water for about 30 seconds. Take the tomato out and then place it in ice water. Cut out the tomato stem and from that end, start peeling the tomato — it should come off easily. To seed the tomato, cut the fruit in half horizontally (not through the stem) and squeeze out the jelly-like seedy sections. Depending on the tomato and what you're making, you may want to save the juice that you squeeze out.

FROM THE KITCHEN OF
**ANTHONY
CARROZZA**

TIKIL GOMEN (ETHIOPIAN VEGETABLE STEW)

Serves 4 to 6

1/2 cup	vegetable oil	125 mL
2 cups	diced onions	500 mL
10	small carrots, diced and parboiled for 10 minutes	10
1 1/2 tsp	salt	7 mL
6	medium potatoes, diced and parboiled 15 minutes	6
3 tbsp	minced garlic	45 mL
1 tsp	turmeric	5 mL
1 tsp	minced ginger root	5 mL
3	green onions, thinly sliced	3
1 cup	vegetable stock or water	250 mL
1	medium savoy cabbage, chopped	1
1/2 tsp	black pepper	2 mL
2	basil leaves, chopped	2
1/2 tsp	black cumin	2 mL

Savoy cabbage has attractive green ruffled leaves and is sometimes called curly cabbage. Unlike green and red cabbage, the leaves are loose with a crinkled texture, a milder flavor and a more tender bite.

If you'd rather not parboil the vegetables, simply cook the stew for a longer period of time.

1. In a large pot, heat oil over medium heat. Add onions, carrots and salt; cook until slightly softened. Add potatoes, garlic, turmeric, ginger and green onions; cook for 2 minutes until all vegetables are coated with spices. Add stock and cook for 15 minutes or until vegetables become tender and liquid begins to evaporate. (You may need to add a little more stock, depending on how large you dice your vegetables and how soft they were after being parboiled.)

2. Add cabbage and stir gently until tender. Season to taste with salt, black pepper, basil and black cumin.

FROM THE KITCHEN OF
ASSEFA KEBEDE

SIDE DISHES

BRANDYWINE TOMATO GRANITÉ

Serves 4

1 cup	strained Brandywine purée (from about 1 lb [500 g] ripe tomatoes)	250 mL
1/2 tsp	lemon juice	2 mL
1/2 tbsp	simple syrup (see box, below)	7 mL
	Sea salt and black pepper to taste	
	Fresh herbs (optional)	

1. Combine all ingredients in a shallow pan and stir. Place in freezer, stirring occasionally.

2. To serve, simply shave off the granité and garnish with fresh herbs if desired.

This granité is a mid-course palate cleanser and will add a bit of sophistication to your meal.

Despite its name, there is no brandy or wine in this recipe. Brandywine tomatoes are an heirloom variety considered to be one of the best tasting tomatoes in North America – intensely sweet and rich. This thin-skinned fruit weighs about 1 lb (500 g) and has a ribbed, irregular shape with many cracks. Because they split so easily, Brandywine tomatoes are extremely difficult to ship so they generally only get as far as the local farmers' market. There are pink, yellow and red Brandywine tomatoes, however the latter two are most common.

FROM THE KITCHEN OF
**JEFF BRANDT,
TIM D'SOUZA AND
STEVE SONG**

To make a simple syrup, combine 2 tbsp (25 mL) white sugar with 2 tbsp (25 mL) water in a saucepan. Bring to a boil, stirring to make sure the sugar is dissolved. Remove from heat.

Serves 4

SPICY CORN FRITTERS WITH APPLES AND GINGER-CINNAMON MAPLE SYRUP

Quebec is the leading maple syrup processor, making 80 million quarts (90.4 million L) of syrup annually. To produce 1 quart (1 L) of syrup, 30 to 40 quarts (34 to 45 L) of sap must be collected and then boiled down. Sap is collected early in the year when the days are warm so the sap flows but the nights are cold so the trees won't bud. Sugar maple trees must be about 40 years old before they will produce sap and each tree can produce between 15 to 40 gallons (68 to 181 L) per season. While it is uncommon that maple trees are sprayed with chemicals, organic maple syrup is certified for the processing of the sap as well.

For directions on roasting peppers, see ANTIPASTO MARINARA *(recipe, page 38).*

1 cup	maple syrup	250 mL
1	1-inch (2.5 cm) piece ginger root, peeled and diced	1
1	cinnamon stick	1
4	tart, hard but juicy apples (Northern Spy, Spartan, Idared, etc.), julienned	4
1 tsp	lemon juice	5 mL
3 cups	corn kernels	750 mL
4	roasted jalapeno peppers, chopped	4
1	roasted red bell pepper, chopped	1
1/2 tsp	salt	2 mL
	White pepper to taste	
3 tbsp	all-purpose flour	45 mL
	Clarified butter and oil for frying	

1. In a saucepan combine maple syrup with ginger and cinnamon; heat until simmering. Turn off heat and let steep for 1 hour. Strain. Reheat when ready to serve fritters.

2. Toss julienned apples with lemon juice to prevent them from browning. Set aside until fritters are ready.

3. In a food processor, purée corn; transfer to a bowl. Add jalapeno and red peppers. Season to taste with salt and pepper. Gradually sprinkle in the flour, whisking constantly.

4. Heat a cast-iron skillet until it is smoking. Add equal amounts of clarified butter and oil. Carefully drop spoonfuls of batter into the hot oil. When the edges are brown and crispy, gently turn fritters over. Cook about 2 minutes per side, watching that the oil stays at a constant temperature. Drain on paper towels.

5. Serve fritters warm with julienned apples on top and maple syrup drizzled all around.

FROM THE KITCHEN OF
LISA SLATER

**Makes about
20 croquettes**

WILD RICE CROQUETTES

*ere is one
way to cook
the 1/2 cup (125 mL)
raw wild rice — which will
produce 1 1/2 to 2 cups
(375 to 500 mL) — for this
recipe. Rinse the rice well
and add 1 1/2 cups (375
mL) salted water. Bring the
water to a boil and reduce
the heat to medium-low
and simmer covered, for 45
to 60 minutes, depending
on the length of grains and
desired doneness. Check the
rice after 40 to 45 min-
utes. If you prefer your wild
rice chewy, about half of the
grains should be cracked.
If you prefer it less
al dente, cook it a little
longer until two-thirds of
the grains are cracked.*

*To make the basmati rice
in this recipe, add 1 1/2
cups (375 mL) salted
water to 1 cup (250 mL)
raw rice. Bring to a boil
and then simmer about
20 minutes. Do not stir.*

FROM THE KITCHEN OF
BRYAN DAVIDSON

PREHEAT OVEN TO 325° F (160° C)

I cup	white basmati rice	250 mL
1/2 cup	wild rice	125 mL
I cup	bread crumbs	250 mL
1/2 cup	brown rice flour	125 mL
3	eggs	3
I	jalapeno pepper, seeded and minced	I
2	cobs corn, kernels only (or I cup [250 mL] frozen)	2
Quarter	bunch coriander, chopped	Quarter
1/2 tbsp	chili powder	7 mL
Half	red bell pepper, finely diced	Half
	Salt	

1. Cook basmati and wild rice separately. (See instructions at left.) Cool.

2. In a bowl combine bread crumbs, flour and cooked
wild and basmati rice. Add eggs, jalapeno pepper,
corn, coriander, chili powder, red pepper and salt;
mix well.

3. Form mixture into 2-inch (5 cm) patties about
1/2 inch (1 cm) thick. Bake on a greased cookie
sheet for about 15 minutes or until golden brown.

Serves 4 to 6

THAI-MARINATED VEGETABLES

All of the ingredients used here can be found in Asian markets and even some supermarkets. Chinese eggplants are long, narrow and violet or lavender in color. They have a sweeter taste and fewer seeds than other eggplants. Fish sauce is made from fermenting dried, salted fish. It is very salty, so season the dish accordingly. Lemon grass is an aromatic herb with thin blades. The lower, tender stem can be chopped or sliced, or the whole stalk can be bruised. Both lemon grass and kaffir lime leaves lend a citrusy tang to a dish. Galangal has a peppery-ginger taste. It has a thinner root than ginger, with pink buds and a yellowish peel.

FROM THE KITCHEN OF
STEWART WEBB &
DAVID EAGLESHAM

MARINADE

I tsp	chopped ginger root	5 mL
I tsp	chopped garlic	5 mL
2/3 cup	extra virgin olive oil	150 mL
4 tsp	sesame oil	20 mL
4 tsp	rice vinegar	20 mL
I	stalk lemon grass	I
2	kaffir lime leaves	2
I tsp	chopped galangal	5 mL
1/2 tsp	fish sauce	2 mL
I tsp	unsweetened shredded coconut	5 mL
1/2 tsp	black pepper	2 mL
	Salt to taste	

VEGETABLES

I cup	shiitake and/or oyster mushrooms, lightly sautéed	250 mL
I	red bell pepper, cut into bite-size pieces	I
2	green onions, cut into pieces	2
2	Chinese eggplants, sliced and grilled or sautéed	2
Half	bunch rapini, blanched and cut into pieces	Half
6	leaves baby bok choy	6

1. In a bowl combine all marinade ingredients; mix well.
2. In another bowl, combine mushrooms, red pepper, green onions, eggplants, rapini and bok choy. Pour marinade over vegetables and marinate for at least 24 hours.

Serves 4 to 6

FIDDLEHEADS, ASPARAGUS AND WILD MUSHROOMS IN ROASTED RED PEPPER VINAIGRETTE

Fiddlehead season is very short, so make the most of these wild delicacies when you can. (They do freeze well, however.) Depending on the region, these unfurled ferns are available between April and July and are eaten raw or cooked. Crunchy and fresh-tasting (similar to asparagus), fiddleheads should be small, tightly curled, jade green in color and firm.

For directions on roasting peppers, see ANTIPASTO MARINARA *(recipe, page 38).*

2 oz	oyster mushrooms, cleaned and sliced	50 g
2 oz	chanterelles, cleaned and sliced	50 g
4 oz	fresh fiddleheads, blanched	125 g
6	asparagus, blanched and briefly grilled (just until grill marks show)	6
1	roasted red bell pepper, peeled and seeded	1
1/2 cup	light olive oil	125 mL
1/4 cup	herbed vinaigrette	50 mL
2	shallots, thinly sliced	2
1 tbsp	chopped mixed herbs	15 mL
	Mixed greens	

1. In a nonstick frying pan, sauté mushrooms. Season with salt and pepper. Remove from heat; mix in the fiddleheads and asparagus.

2. In a food processor, purée roasted red pepper. Add olive oil, herbed vinaigrette, shallots and herbs. Pour over mushrooms, fiddleheads and asparagus.

3. Serve over a bed of mixed greens.

FROM THE KITCHEN OF
BRAD CLEASE

PATTYPAN SQUASH FILLED WITH ROUILLE

Serves 4 to 8

1	roasted red bell pepper peeled and seeded	1
1	egg yolk (at room temperature)	1
2	cloves garlic	2
	Juice of half lemon	
3/4 cup	virgin olive oil	175 mL
1/2 tsp	salt	2 mL
Pinch	cayenne pepper	Pinch
	Fresh black pepper to taste	
Pinch	saffron (optional)	Pinch
8	pattypan squash, bottoms trimmed flat and insides scooped out with a melon baller or 2 or 3 green or yellow zucchini cut into 2-inch [5 cm] pieces with the middle scooped out	8
8	basil leaves for garnish	8

1. Make the *rouille*: In a food processor, purée roasted red pepper, egg yolk, garlic and 1 tsp (5 mL) lemon juice. With the motor running, add olive oil slowly in a stream just until mixture begins to thicken. Add salt, cayenne pepper, black pepper and, if using, saffron. With motor running, add remaining oil and lemon juice. Taste and adjust seasoning.

2. Blanch pattypan squash in boiling salted water for 1 1/2 minutes. Refresh in cold water and pat dry with paper towel.

3. Fill each squash with *rouille* and serve garnished with a basil leaf.

The pattypan squash's scalloped edge adds a nice visual touch to this side dish. About 3 inches (7.5 cm) in diameter, this saucer-shaped summer squash comes in shades of white, yellow and pale green.

Saffron is one of the most expensive spices in the world and one of the oldest. It comes from the stigma of a certain type of crocus and is hand-picked and dried. Approximately 250,000 stigma are needed to make 1 lb (500 g). Buy whole saffron filaments; the powdered version can be adulterated with cheaper spices. Only a pinch is necessary to flavor any dish.

For directions on roasting peppers, see ANTIPASTO MARINARA *(recipe, page 38).*

FROM THE KITCHEN OF
JEFF DUECK

Variation

Grill the pattypan over high heat to give it a bit more flavor and grill marks.

CHEDDAR BREAD PUDDING WITH MAPLE, DRIED CHERRY AND WALNUT COMPOTE

Serves 6 to 8

13- BY 9-INCH (3 L) BAKING DISH, BUTTERED

BREAD PUDDING

2 tbsp	unsalted butter	25 mL
2	leeks, white and light green parts only, cut into 1/4-inch (5 mm) rings, washed and drained	2
10	large eggs	10
3 cups	whipping (35%) cream	750 mL
1 tsp	salt	5 mL
1/4 tsp	freshly ground pepper	1 mL
8 oz	sourdough bread, sliced 1 inch (2.5 cm) thick and toasted	250 g
1 lb	Cheddar, grated	500 g

COMPOTE

1 cup	maple syrup	250 mL
1	sprig rosemary	1
1/4 cup	dried cherries	50 mL
1/4 cup	toasted walnuts	50 mL

1. Bread pudding: In a skillet melt butter over low heat. Add leeks and cook until soft. Allow to cool. In a bowl, whisk together eggs, cream, salt and pepper.

2. Arrange one layer of bread in prepared baking dish. Sprinkle with half the Cheddar and half the leeks. Arrange second layer of bread. Sprinkle with remaining cheese and leeks. Pour egg mixture over bread pudding to cover completely. Refrigerate for 1 hour or overnight.

3. Bake in a preheated 375° F (190° C) oven, uncovered, for about 40 minutes or until golden and bubbling.

4. Compote: In a saucepan over very low heat, warm maple syrup with rosemary for 2 to 3 minutes. Stir in cherries and walnuts. Serve with bread pudding, warm or at room temperature.

Dried cherries provide an incredibly intense cherry flavor that works well in sauces, baked goods, granola and grain dishes — or when eaten on their own like raisins. While fresh cherries have a short season, dried cherries are available throughout the year in health-food and specialty stores. Most dried cherries are made from the sweet Bing variety.

A number of dried fruits are now available organically, including cherries, apricots, peaches, pears, apples and raisins.

FROM THE KITCHEN OF
SUZANNE BABY

Makes 6 tartlettes

GOAT CHEESE AND LEEK TARTLETTE WITH A WILD RICE CRUST

Wild rice, which is available organically, has an earthy, nutty flavor, a chewy texture and a smoky scent. Not actually a rice at all, it is the grain of an aquatic grass native to the Great Lakes region. Grown in marshes and shallow, muddy banks along fresh-water lakes, wild rice is highly nutritious but expensive. The traditional method of gathering wild rice, which is still used by some harvesters today, entails poling a boat through the water, bending the stalks over the boat and shaking the ripe ones to dislodge the grains. As nature would have it, the grains do not ripen at the same time so the harvesters often have to go back for a second and third threshing.

For directions on cooking wild rice, see WILD RICE CROQUETTES (recipe, page 140).

FROM THE KITCHEN OF
JASON WORTZMAN

PREHEAT OVEN TO 350° F (180° C)
SIX 4-INCH (10 CM) TART TINS, BUTTERED

1	large sweet potato, peeled and thinly sliced	1
1	small leek, white part only, washed and diced	1
1 tbsp	butter	15 mL
4 oz	soft goat cheese	125 g
2/3 cup	whipping (35%) cream	150 mL
2	eggs, beaten	2
1/2 tsp	salt	2 mL
1/4 tsp	pepper	1 mL
1 cup	cooked wild rice	250 mL
1	egg, beaten	1
1	green onion, finely chopped	1
	Fresh cooked asparagus	
	Roasted red pepper strips	
	Fried leeks	

1. Line the tart tins with overlapping pieces of sweet potato.

2. Sauté leek in butter until soft; let cool.

3. In a food processor or blender, purée goat cheese. Gradually add cream; blend until smooth. Transfer to a bowl. Stir in the 2 beaten eggs, leeks, salt and pepper. Pour mixture into tart shells and bake for 15 minutes or until center rises and is just firm. Let cool slightly.

4. In a bowl mix together the wild rice, 1 egg and green onion. Cover the tops of the cooled tartlettes with wild rice topping. Bake for another 10 to 12 minutes or until topping has set.

5. Garnish with fresh cooked asparagus, roasted red pepper strips and fried leeks.

GRILLED POLENTA WITH TOMATILLO CORN SALSA

Serves 6 to 8

The tomatillo is most often used in Mexican dishes — especially salsa verde. Resembling a green cherry tomato wrapped in a beige paper-lanternlike husk, it looks like and is related to the Cape gooseberry. The tomatillo is acidic and slightly gelatinous and has a lemony flavor. Usually cooked in traditional dishes, it can be eaten raw. Look for firm, dry, unhusked tomatillos in specialty grocers and Latin American markets.

9- BY 5-INCH (2 L) TERRINE OR LOAF PAN LINED WITH PLASTIC WRAP

TOMATILLO SALSA

4	tomatillos, sliced (or chopped)	4
I	cob sweet corn, blanched	I
Quarter	red onion, finely diced	Quarter
Quarter	red bell pepper, julienned	Quarter
Half	jalapeno, finely diced	Half
3 tbsp	white wine vinegar	45 mL
1/2 tsp	garlic purée	2 mL
	Juice of I lime	
1/3 cup	extra virgin olive oil	75 mL

POLENTA

I 1/4 cup	chicken stock *or* vegetable stock	300 mL
I 1/4 cup	whipping (35%) cream	300 mL
I tbsp	garlic purée	15 mL
2 tbsp	basil purée	25 mL
I tbsp	chopped thyme	15 mL
I tsp	jalapeno purée	5 mL
I tsp	salt	5 mL
1/4 tsp	cayenne pepper	I mL
2 cups	cornmeal	500 mL
	Cornmeal for dredging	

1. Salsa: In a bowl combine all salsa ingredients; mix well and refrigerate overnight.

2. Polenta: In a pot combine stock, cream, garlic, basil, thyme, jalapeno, salt and cayenne pepper; bring to a boil. Gradually add cornmeal, stirring constantly. Mixture should have a firm texture; adjust as required with more liquid or more cornmeal. Pour mixture into a terrine and refrigerate for at least 1 hour.

3. To serve: Preheat barbecue or grill. Cut polenta into 1/2-inch (1 cm) slices and dredge in cornmeal. Place on barbecue and grill both sides. Spoon salsa on top.

FROM THE KITCHEN OF
ANTHONY NUTH

BREADS

Makes 12
open-faced
biscuits

CORN AND SAGE BISCUITS WITH GRILLED LEEK BUTTER, SHIITAKES AND PLUM CONFIT

PREHEAT OVEN TO 350° F (180° C)

Tamarind, or "date of India" as it's also called, comes from a towering tree that grows in tropical climates. The brown pods are about 3 to 5 inches (7.5 to 15 cm) long and contain dark, shiny seeds from which the fleshy, acidic tamarind pulp is extracted. Tamarind can be bought as pods, pulp or paste in some health-food, Asian and Latin American stores. Often hot water is needed to soften the tamarind pulp before using.

BISCUITS

2 cups	all-purpose flour	500 mL
1 1/2 tbsp	baking powder	20 mL
1 1/2 tbsp	sugar	20 mL
Pinch	salt	Pinch
3 oz	butter	75 g
1/3 cup	corn kernels, blanched	75 mL
1 tsp	chopped sage	5 mL
3/4 cup	buttermilk	175 mL

GRILLED LEEK BUTTER AND SHIITAKES

PREHEAT BARBECUE OR GRILL

Half	bunch leeks, white part only, well washed	Half
	Extra virgin olive oil	
2 tbsp	softened butter	25 mL
1	lemon	1
	Salt and pepper to taste	
12	large shiitake mushrooms, washed and trimmed	12

SWEET-AND-SOUR PLUM CONFIT

1/2 tbsp	honey	7 mL
1/2 tbsp	sugar	7 mL
1/2 tbsp	water	7 mL
Half	stalk lemon grass	Half
1 1/2 lbs	prune plums, peeled (peels reserved) and pitted	750 g
1 tsp	minced shallots	5 mL
1/2 tsp	rice vinegar *or* dry sherry	2 mL
1/2 tsp	red wine vinegar	2 mL
1/4 tsp	Dijon mustard	1 mL
1/2 tbsp	tamarind purée	7 mL
1 1/2 tbsp	extra virgin olive oil	20 mL
Pinch	salt	Pinch
1	lemon	1

FROM THE KITCHEN OF
GARY HOYER

1. Biscuits: In a bowl sift together the flour, baking powder, sugar and salt. Cut in butter until it is the size of small peas. Make a well in the center of the mixture. In a bowl mix together corn, sage and buttermilk; pour into well in biscuit mixture; mix until combined but still crumbly (don't overmix). On a floured board, roll out mixture until 3/4 inch (1.5 cm) thick. Cut into 2 1/2-inch (6 cm) squares. Bake on a greased cookie sheet for about 30 minutes until golden brown and slightly springy.

2. Leek butter: In a pot of boiling salted water, blanch leeks for 3 minutes; drain. Brush grill with oil; grill leeks over high heat for about 1 1/2 minutes on each side. Remove and chop finely; blend into butter. Season with a drop of lemon juice, salt and pepper.

3. Shiitakes: In preheated 400° F (200° C) oven, partially cook shiitakes for about 3 minutes. Brush grill with oil; grill mushrooms for 2 minutes on each side. Season with a few drops of lemon juice, salt and pepper and brush lightly with oil.

4. Confit: In a saucepan combine honey, sugar and water; bring to a boil. Bruise the lemon grass and put in a cheesecloth sack along with reserved plum skins; add to sugar syrup, along with pitted plums. Reduce heat and simmer, covered, for 15 minutes. Remove from heat and blend in remaining ingredients; add lemon last to taste. Adjust seasoning.

5. To serve: Cut warm biscuits in half. Spread with the grilled leek butter and dab with plum confit. Top with a warm shiitake mushroom and dab on a bit more plum confit.

**Makes
1 focaccia**

YUKON GOLD POTATO FOCACCIA WITH PARMESAN AND FRESH CHIVES

aker's yeast is a microscopic fungus that ferments the sugars found in flour to produce carbon dioxide. The gluten in the flour traps the gas, which leavens the dough. When the bread is baking, the trapped carbon dioxide creates air pockets, giving the bread its light-ness. Active dry yeast is sold in envelopes and in bulk. Keep dry yeast refrig-erated and, for the best results, do not use yeast past its expiry date.

PREHEAT OVEN TO 450° F (230° C)

1/2 cup	water (at room temperature)	125 mL
1/2 cup	milk	125 mL
6 tbsp	olive oil	90 mL
1	envelope dry yeast	1
2 3/4 cups	hard bread flour	675 mL
1 tsp	fine sea salt	5 mL
1	large Yukon Gold potato (or other yellow-fleshed potato), sliced as thinly as possible	1
	Olive oil	
	Salt and freshly ground pepper	
1 tbsp	chopped chives	15 mL
1/4 cup	freshly grated Parmesan cheese	50 mL

1. In a bowl stir together the water, milk and olive oil. Break up yeast and whisk it into the liquid. Let stand for 10 minutes.

2. Add flour and salt to a food processor fitted with a blade. Add yeast mixture and process for a few seconds. Let dough rest in the processor for 15 minutes.

3. Continue mixing dough for 15 to 20 seconds or until a smooth consistency is reached. Remove from processor and place in a lightly oiled bowl. Allow to rise, covered, for about 2 hours at room temperature.

4. Deflate the dough. Press the edges of the dough into the center, invert, and tuck in short ends to form a rough oval. Place the dough on an oiled cookie sheet and allow to rise for 2 hours, covered.

5. Dimple the dough with your fingertips, leaving a border. Place potato slices in overlapping rows on the dough. Drizzle with olive oil; add salt and pepper to taste. Sprinkle with chives and cheese. Bake for 30 minutes until top and bottom are golden brown and crisp. Remove to a cooling rack.

FROM THE KITCHEN OF
ANDREA DAMON
GIBSON

Makes 2 flatbreads

FLATBREAD

Chef Ennest developed this flatbread to accompany his RED LENTIL HUMMUS (see recipe, page 27).

There are hundreds of flatbreads made around the world, some of them using yeast, sourdough starter or no leavener whatsoever. Tortillas, rotis, pitas, focaccia and naan are among the more popular flatbreads.

PREHEAT OVEN TO 400° F (200° C)

1 cup	warm water	250 mL
1/2 tbsp	dry yeast	7 mL
1 tbsp	granulated sugar	15 mL
1/4 cup	olive oil	50 mL
2 tsp	salt	10 mL
2 tbsp	flax seed	25 mL
2 cups	all-purpose flour	500 mL
1/4 cup	whole wheat flour	50 mL
	Olive oil	

1. In a large bowl, hydrate yeast in warm water by letting it sit for 5 minutes.

2. Add remaining ingredients and knead for 3 minutes. (At this point, the dough should be tacky but not stick to the bowl, work surface or hands; if necessary, add more flour or water to achieve this consistency.) Knead dough for another 3 minutes; cover and let rise for 20 minutes.

3. Divide dough into 2 pieces and roll into balls. With a rolling pin, roll dough to 1/4- to 1/2-inch (5 mm to 1 cm) thickness, depending on whether you prefer a thin or thick flatbread.

4. Prick dough with a fork and brush with olive oil. Bake for 10 minutes. Cut into wedges and serve.

Variation

Sprinkle some fresh herbs on the flatbread after you've brushed on the olive oil.

IRISH WHEATEN BREAD

Makes 1 loaf

PREHEAT OVEN TO 450° F (230° C)

9- BY 5-INCH (2 L) LOAF PAN, LIGHTLY OILED

2 cups	whole wheat flour	500 mL
I cup	bran	250 mL
1/2 cup	pinhead oats *or* regular oats	125 mL
I tsp	baking soda, sifted	5 mL
I tsp	salt	5 mL
I	egg	I
2 tbsp	vegetable oil	25 mL
2 tbsp	molasses	25 mL
I 1/4 cups	buttermilk	300 mL

1. In a large bowl, mix together the flour, bran, oats, baking soda and salt; be sure to blend the baking soda throughout.

2. In a separate bowl, whisk together egg, oil, molasses and buttermilk.

3. Make a well in the center of the dry ingredients. Add wet ingredients all at once; mix gently but thoroughly. (A clean, claw-shaped hand works best; use only one hand, however, keeping the other hand clean for such inevitable tasks as answering the phone, opening the oven door, turning on the tap, etc.)

4. Transfer mixture to pan and immediately place in hot oven. Bake at 450° F (230° C) for 15 minutes. Reduce temperature to 375° F (190° C) and bake for another 35 minutes or until loaf is brown and sounds hollow when tapped on the bottom. Cool on a wire rack.

Buttermilk was once the milky byproduct left over from the traditional butter-making process, but is no longer. Today bacterial cultures are added to pasteurized milk, which turns the lactose into lactic acid, giving the buttermilk its tang. This thick, creamy milk is often sold in 1 quart (1 L) cartons; if you can't use all of the buttermilk by its expiry date, it freezes well for up to 1 month.

You can also make your own buttermilk: just mix 1 tbsp (15 mL) lemon juice or vinegar with 1 cup less 1 tbsp (235 mL) milk to make 1 cup (250 mL) buttermilk. Let stand for 10 minutes.

Variation

Add dried fruit, such as currants or raisins, to the batter.

FROM THE KITCHEN OF
**ADRIENNE
O'CALLAGHAN**

Serves 8

TOASTED PECAN-ORANGE TEA BREAD

If possible, use organic citrus fruits in recipes that call for orange, lemon or lime zest. Conventional citrus fruits are heavily sprayed with pesticides, treated with fungicides and coated with waxes. If organic citrus is not available, be sure to wash the fruit very well.

Toasting the pecans before adding them to the batter accentuates the nuttiness of the bread. To toast pecans, lay them flat on a tray and bake for about 5 to 8 minutes at 350° F (180° C).

PREHEAT OVEN TO 350° F (180° C)

9- BY 5-INCH (2 L) LOAF PAN, GREASED

1/2 cup	unsalted butter, softened	125 mL
1 cup	granulated sugar	250 mL
2	eggs	2
1 tsp	vanilla extract	5 mL
2 cups	all-purpose flour	500 mL
1 tsp	baking powder	5 mL
1/2 tsp	salt	2 mL
1/2 tsp	cinnamon	2 mL
1 cup	sour cream	250 mL
1 tsp	baking soda	5 mL
3/4 cup	toasted pecans, chopped	175 mL
	Zest of 1 orange	

1. In a bowl cream butter and sugar until smooth and light in color. Blend in eggs and vanilla.

2. In a bowl, blend flour, baking powder, salt and cinnamon. In another bowl, blend sour cream and baking soda. Stirring after each addition, add half of the dry ingredients to the egg batter, then the sour cream mixture, and then the remaining dry ingredients.

3. Mix in pecans and orange zest; pour into prepared loaf pan. Bake for about 1 hour, until a toothpick inserted into the center comes out clean and dry.

FROM THE KITCHEN OF
DAINA PAULIUS

HAZELNUT BREAD WITH FRESH CHEESE AND MAPLE-ROASTED PEARS

Between the main event and dessert, a sampling of well-made cheese, good bread and seasonal fruits adds luxury to an elegant dinner. Here all 3 components are served slightly warm.

Hazelnuts are also called filberts because many of the nuts are ready for harvesting for the feast day St. Philbert. A foliated membrane partially covers each shell and must be removed in order to get to the hazelnut. After toasting hazelnuts, the thin skin covering the nuts can be easily rubbed off in a clean cloth.

FROM THE KITCHEN OF
ANDREA DAMON GIBSON

FRESH CHEESE

2 cups	goat's milk yogurt	500 mL

HAZELNUT BREAD

PREHEAT OVEN TO 500° F (260° C) FOR 1 HOUR BEFORE BAKING

3/4 cup	water at room temperature	175 mL
1 tsp	dry yeast	5 mL
1 1/2 cups	hard bread flour	375 mL
1 1/2 tbsp	rye flour	20 mL
1 tsp	sea salt	5 mL
1 cup	roasted hazelnuts, coarsely chopped	250 mL
	Cornmeal for sprinkling	
	Flour for dusting	

MAPLE-ROASTED PEARS

PREHEAT OVEN TO 350° F (180° C)

3	pears, peeled, cored and halved	3
	Juice of half lemon	
2 tbsp	unsalted butter	25 mL
1/4 cup	maple syrup	50 mL

1. Fresh cheese: Place goat's milk yogurt in a sieve over a bowl. Let drain overnight in the refrigerator. In a bowl with an electric mixer, whip cheese to a smooth consistency. Set aside.

2. Hazelnut bread: In a bowl stir together water and yeast. Cover and let stand 5 minutes until it becomes creamy. In the bowl of a food processor fitted with a steel blade, combine flours and salt. Add yeast mixture and pulse several times until the dough forms a ball. Let the motor run for about 25 seconds. The dough will be sticky.

3. On a floured surface, knead dough several times by hand. Form into a ball. Place dough into a lightly oiled bowl and cover at room temperature for 1 1/2 to 2 hours.

4. Gently deflate the dough and carefully knead in hazelnuts. The dough will form a ball naturally. Place the round loaf onto a cookie sheet sprinkled with cornmeal. Cover and allow to proof at room temperature for 1 1/2 to 2 hours.

5. Sprinkle loaf with water. Dust with flour and make several slashes 1/2 inch (1 cm) deep in the top of the dough with a serrated knife. Reduce oven temperature to 450° F (230° C) and bake for 40 to 45 minutes. Allow to cool completely on a rack.

6. Maple-roasted pears: Toss the prepared pears with the lemon juice. In an ovenproof saucepan, melt butter over medium heat. Add pears and cook until browned. Pour maple syrup over. Place saucepan, uncovered, in preheated oven; roast for 5 minutes. Turn pears and roast for another 5 minutes or until tender. Remove from oven; slice thinly and keep warm.

7. To serve: Cut hazelnut bread into 1/2-inch (1cm) slices. Toast or grill the bread lightly on both sides. Cut the slices into strips or points. Top with fresh cheese and allow to melt slightly. Place pear slice on cheese and serve immediately.

DESSERTS

GREEN APPLE AND RASPBERRY SEMI-FREDDO IN A CORN FLOUR TART

Serves 6 to 8

PREHEAT OVEN TO 350° F (180° C)

9-INCH (22.5 CM) FLAN SHELL

CORN FLOUR TART

1/2 cup	butter	125 mL
1/3 cup	granulated sugar	75 mL
1 tbsp	water	15 mL
1/2 tsp	vanilla extract	2 mL
1	egg white	1
1/2 cup	all-purpose flour	125 mL
3/4 cup	corn flour	175 mL
1/4 cup	cornmeal	50 mL
1/2 tsp	baking soda	2 mL
1/2 tsp	salt	2 mL

GREEN APPLE SEMI-FREDDO

2	green apples, peeled, cored and puréed	2
1	egg yolk	1
1/2 cup	granulated sugar	125 mL
1 cup	whipping (35%) cream, whipped	250 mL
1 pint	raspberries	500 mL
	Sugar to taste	
	Whipped cream (optional)	

This is a light and refreshing dessert for a hot summer day. The corn flour and corn-meal in the pastry add a wonderful flavor and texture to the tart.

When raspberries and apples are being puréed, leave small chunks of fruit for texture. Any type of tart apple – such as Granny Smith, Idared or Northern Spy – will work with this recipe.

To blind bake, line the inside of the pastry with parchment paper or aluminum foil. Add ceramic baking weights or raw dried beans or rice (which can be reused many times) to fill the tart.

FROM THE KITCHEN OF
LORENE SAURO

1. Corn flour tart: In a bowl cream butter and sugar together until smooth. Add water, vanilla extract and egg white. In another bowl, combine flours, corn-meal, baking soda and salt; add to butter mixture; mix well. Chill for 1 hour.

2. On a lightly floured surface, roll out the dough to fit the flan shell. Blind bake (see note at left) for 20 minutes until golden around the edges. Remove from oven and let cool.

3. Green apple semi-freddo: In a double boiler, combine green apples, yolk and sugar; heat gently over simmering water, stirring occasionally, for about 15 minutes or until mixture is hot to the touch. Let cool to room temperature. Fold whipped cream into apple mixture. Spoon semi-freddo into tart shell and freeze.

4. To finish: Purée raspberries in a food processor; add sugar to taste. Remove semi-freddo from freezer 15 to 20 minutes before serving. Serve with raspberry purée and, if desired, whipped cream.

Variation

Spread the raspberry purée on top of the tart before serving and garnish with edible flowers.

FROM THE KITCHEN OF
ADRIENNE
O'CALLAGHAN

Makes 1 tart

CRANBERRY TOFFEE TART

Fresh and dried cranberries, white chocolate and toasted hazelnuts are partnered with a toffee mixture to create this delicious dessert.

Most of this recipe can be prepared ahead of time: The unrolled pastry dough may be kept wrapped and refrigerated for 2 days. The tart shell can be baked the day before serving and kept covered at room temperature. The toffee mixture can also be made up to 5 days in advance of baking, then stored in a covered container in the refrigerator and brought to room temperature before using.

PREHEAT OVEN TO 375° F (190° C)
9-INCH (2.5 L) TART PAN (PREFERABLY ONE WITH
A REMOVABLE BOTTOM) OR FLAN RING

PASTRY

4 oz	cold unsalted butter	125 g
	Juice and zest of 1 orange	
2 tsp	ice water	10 mL
1 cup	unbleached all-purpose flour	250 mL
2 tsp	granulated sugar	10 mL
1 tbsp	chopped fresh rosemary	15 mL
1/4 tsp	salt	1 mL

FILLING

1/2 cup	sugar	125 mL
1 cup	light corn syrup	250 mL
2 tbsp	unsalted butter	25 mL
3	large eggs	3
1 tsp	vanilla extract	5 mL
2 oz	high-quality white chocolate, chopped into small pieces	50 g
3/4 cup	toasted and skinned hazelnuts, chopped coarsely	175 mL
1/2 cup	fresh cranberries	125 mL
1/2 cup	dried cranberries	125 mL

1. Pastry: Cut butter into 1/2-inch (1 cm) cubes; refrigerate. In a measuring cup, stir together 1 tbsp (15 mL) of the orange juice with the ice water. Refrigerate.

2. In a large bowl, mix together flour, sugar, rosemary, orange zest and salt. Add chilled, cubed butter and shake to coat each cube with flour mixture. Transfer to a food processor and pulse the motor on and off about 15 times until the butter particles are the size of small peas.

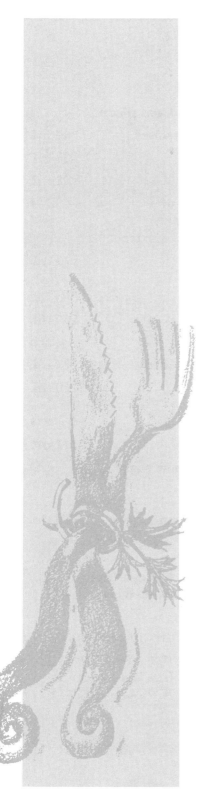

3. With the motor running, add cold juice mixture all at once; process about 10 seconds. (Alternatively, rub or cut in the butter by hand and add the liquid.) Check the dough; it should just hold together when pinched. Add a little more liquid if necessary. Turn dough onto a sheet of aluminum foil and press together gently. (Handle dough as little as possible for a more tender pastry.) Refrigerate at least 30 minutes.

4. Roll the dough out to a thickness of 1/4 to 3/8 inch (5 to 7 mm) and fit into tart pan or flan ring. Prick with a fork and chill 20 minutes.

5. Cover dough with aluminum foil or parchment paper and fill with weights (dried rice and beans or ceramic baking weights). Bake the weighted dough for 20 minutes; remove weights and foil and let cool.

6. Filling: In a heavy skillet, melt sugar over medium heat, stirring constantly until completely melted and a deep golden brown. Remove from heat; add corn syrup. (Be careful: the mixture will seize up, bubble and splatter.) Return pan to heat and cook mixture until smooth. Add butter; stir until melted.

7. In a bowl whisk together eggs and vanilla extract until thoroughly mixed. Add caramel mixture in a stream, whisking continuously until well combined.

8. Spread the chocolate, hazelnuts, fresh and dried cranberries into the tart shell, distributing evenly. Pour in toffee mixture to just below the rim of the shell. Make sure that all the fruit and nuts are coated with toffee, gently dunking those that are not coated.

9. Bake for 35 to 40 minutes in the lower-middle level of the oven, until the pastry is browned and the filling is puffed and golden. Cool the tart on a rack. Remove from pan when completely cool.

Makes 1 pie

WILD APPLE, GRAPE, ELDERBERRY AND BLACK RASPBERRY PIE

PREHEAT TO 425° F (220° C)
9-INCH (2.5 L) PIE PAN

Elderberries are tiny indigo-black berries that grow profusely in moist woods, ravines and clearings throughout a large part of North America. The woody elderberry shrub bears clusters of fragrant flowers, which are said to be delicious when dipped into an egg batter and deep-fried like fritters. Although they can be eaten raw, elderberries are most often cooked and used in sauces, jellies, pies, wines and Sambuca liqueur.

FILLING

4	apples, peeled, cored and sliced	4
I cup	grapes, seeded or seedless	250 mL
1/2 cup	elderberries	125 mL
1/2 cup	black raspberries	125 mL
I	2-inch (5 cm) piece of vanilla bean, seeds only *or* I tsp (5 mL) vanilla extract	I
3/4 cup	maple syrup	175 mL

CRUST

2 cups	pastry flour	500 mL
Pinch	salt	Pinch
3/4 cup	butter, chilled and cubed	175 mL
3 to 4 tbsp	ice water	45 to 60 mL
I	egg	I
I tbsp	milk	15 mL
	Maple sugar *or* organic sugar for sprinkling	
I cup	natural or organic apple cider *or* juice (commercial apple juice will not work)	250 mL
	Ice cream *or* CRÈME FRAÎCHE (see recipe, page 62) *or* whipped cream (optional)	

1. Filling: In a medium saucepan over medium heat, combine apples, grapes, elderberries, raspberries and vanilla seeds; cook gently until fruit starts to soften. (If using vanilla extract, add it after cooking fruit.)

FROM THE KITCHEN OF
MICHAEL
STADTLÄNDER

2. In a small saucepan, boil maple syrup until it reduces and darkens slightly in color. (To test, dip a spoon in and out of the syrup. Any drops from the spoon should immediately be thick and gluey.) Add syrup to fruit and mix. (If syrup hardens during this process, it will smooth itself out when the pie is baked.) Let filling cool.

3. Crust: In a food processor, combine flour, salt and butter; process until butter is completely cut into the flour. (Alternatively, you can use a pastry blender.) Add water so that everything sticks together. Chill for about 30 minutes.

4. On a floured surface, roll out half of the pastry and place it in pie pan. Roll out the other half and cut into strips.

5. Pour filling into pie shell. Lay half of the pastry strips over the pie from right to left and then crisscross the other half from top to bottom. Mix egg and milk to make an eggwash; brush over pastry. Sprinkle with sugar. Bake in preheated oven for 20 minutes. Reduce temperature to 350° F (180° C) and bake another 20 minutes.

6. Meanwhile, in a saucepan, boil apple cider until reduced by half. Let cool.

7. When pie has cooled, serve with apple syrup and, if desired, ice cream, crème fraîche or whipped cream.

Makes 1 pie

OKANAGAN PIE WITH SUN-DRIED FRUIT AND BIRCH SYRUP

PREHEAT OVEN TO 400° F (200° C)

9-INCH (2.5 L) PIE PLATE

PASTRY

1/2 cup	butter	125 mL
1/3 cup	sugar	75 mL
1/8 cup	milk	25 mL
1	egg yolk	1
1 1/2 cups	flour	375 mL
1/8 tsp	salt	0.5 mL

Eggwash (unused half of egg used in pie filling [see below] mixed with a bit of water)

Sugar for sprinkling

FILLING

6	Spartan apples, peeled, cored and thinly sliced	6
1/4 cup	sugar	50 mL
Half	egg (use other half for eggwash)	Half
1/4 tsp	salt	1 mL
1/2 tbsp	vanilla extract	7 mL
2 1/2 tbsp	all-purpose flour	35 mL
1/2 tbsp	cinnamon	7 mL

SUN-DRIED FRUIT AND BIRCH SYRUP

1 cup	sugar	250 mL
1/4 cup	orange juice	50 mL
1 cup	apple juice	250 mL
1 cup	assorted sun-dried fruits (raisins, currants cranberries, apricots, etc.)	250 mL
1/2 cup	birch syrup *or* maple syrup *or* molasses	125 mL

1. Pastry: In a bowl cream together butter and sugar until smooth. Add milk and egg yolk; mix in flour and salt until it just comes together. Refrigerate for 2 hours.

This recipe uses an unusual ingredient, Cameron's Birch Syrup from Alaska. Pastry chef Adams says it's thicker and richer than maple syrup, with a molassesy flavor.

When substituting fruits, choose ones that are equal in wetness and texture — for example, substitute pears for apples or apricots for plums.

FROM THE KITCHEN OF
VICTORIA ADAMS

2. Divide pastry into 2 parts. Roll out the first piece to 1/4-inch (5 mm) thickness and place in pie plate.

3. Filling: In a bowl combine apples, sugar, half egg, salt, vanilla, flour and cinnamon; toss until well coated. Place filling into pie shell. Brush pastry around the rim of the pie plate with eggwash.

4. Roll out the second half of the pastry and lay on top of pie plate. Trim any overhang and crimp edges. Brush with eggwash and sprinkle with sugar. Place in the refrigerator for about 30 minutes to set.

5. Bake in preheated oven for 15 to 20 minutes. Reduce oven temperature to 350° F (180° C) and bake for another 30 to 40 minutes.

6. Meanwhile, prepare the sun-dried fruit and birch syrup: In a heavy-bottomed saucepan, combine sugar and orange juice. Bring to a boil; cook until sugar is caramelized to a golden brown. (The mixture will be very hot; use extreme caution when handling.) Slowly add apple juice and whisk until smooth. If juice is cold, caramelized sugar may bubble and spit; just keep it on the heat and it will become smooth. Stir in sun-dried fruits and birch syrup.

7. When pie is ready; remove from oven and serve with fruit-and-syrup mixture.

Makes 1 pie

PEACH-RASPBERRY PIE

Organic butter is becoming more widely available on the market. But for those who are cholesterol-conscious or vegan, raw organic coconut oil is a good alternative. This naturally saturated fat, which has a very subtle coconut flavor, bakes like butter and is an ideal substitute for shortening or butter in pastry (chill the oil first). When baking with coconut oil, you can generally use about 25 percent less fat. Originally used by the indigenous peoples of Polynesia, studies have found that coconut oil is easier to digest than other fats and decreases the chance of heart problems.

PREHEAT OVEN TO 400° F (200° C)
9-INCH (2.5 L) PIE PAN

PASTRY

1 1/8 cups	all-purpose flour	275 mL
1/8 tsp	salt	0.5 mL
1/4 cup	butter	50 mL
1/4 cup	shortening	50 mL
2 tbsp	ice water	125 mL

FILLING

2 tbsp	cornstarch	25 mL
2/3 cup	sugar	150 mL
6	peaches, peeled and sliced	6
1/2 tsp	almond extract	2 mL
1 tsp	orange zest	5 mL
1/2 pint	raspberries	250 mL

CRUMBLE

1/8 cup	soft butter	25 mL
1/4 cup	all-purpose flour	50 mL
1/4 cup	granulated sugar	50 mL
1/4 cup	sliced almonds	50 mL

1. Pastry: In a bowl stir together flour and salt. Cut butter and shortening into the flour with a pastry blender. (This may also be done with a food processor but the butter and shortening must be cold.) Add water and gently mix until dough sticks together. Chill for 30 minutes.

2. On a lightly floured surface, roll out two-thirds of the dough to a 10-inch (25 cm) diameter and place into pie plate. There should be a slight overhang.

FROM THE KITCHEN OF
WANDA BEAVER

3. Filling: In a medium-sized bowl, mix together cornstarch and sugar. Add peaches, almond extract and orange zest and mix. Place in prepared crust. Put raspberries in the center of the peach mixture and press down lightly.

4. Roll out remaining dough and cut into 9 strips, each 1 inch (2.5 cm) wide. Lay 4 strips across the pie from right to left. Lay the remaining strips from top to bottom. Trim off any overhang. Crimp edges.

5. Crumble: With a pastry blender (or your fingertips), mix butter, flour and sugar. Add almonds and sprinkle on pie. Bake in preheated oven for 15 to 20 minutes. Reduce heat to 350° F (180° C) and bake for another 40 minutes.

Serves 8 to 10

FRESH CORN BUTTERCAKE WITH CARAMEL SAUCE AND PEACHES

Peaches originated in China and are considered a symbol of immortality. This sweet and juicy fruit is classified as freestone or clingstone, according to the ease with which the pit separates from the flesh. Because peaches stop ripening once they are picked, choose peaches that are firm but yield gently when pressed, have even coloring with a red blush and are fragrant smelling.

PREHEAT OVEN TO 350° F (180° C)

9-INCH (2.5 L) ROUND PAN

OR TWO 8- BY 4-INCH (1.5 L) LOAF PANS, GREASED AND FLOURED

1 1/2 cups	corn kernels, cooked	375 mL
2/3 cup	milk	150 mL
3/4 cup	butter	175 mL
1 1/2 cups	granulated sugar	375 mL
3 cups	sifted cake and pastry flour	750 mL
1/3 cup	cornmeal	75 mL
4 tsp	baking powder	20 mL
3/4 tsp	salt	4 mL
6	large egg yolks	6
2 1/4 tsp	vanilla extract	11 mL

CARAMEL SAUCE

1 1/2 cups	granulated sugar	375 mL
1/2 cup	water	125 mL
1/2 cup	whipping (35%) cream	125 mL
4	peaches, sliced	4

1. In a food processor or blender, combine corn and milk; process until blended. Strain mixture through a sieve into a bowl; discard solids.

2. In a bowl with an electric mixer, cream together butter and sugar. Add half the corn milk.

3. In a separate bowl, mix flour, cornmeal, baking powder and salt. Add to butter mixture and mix thoroughly, scraping the sides of the bowl. Mix together remaining corn milk with the egg yolks and vanilla. Add to flour-butter mixture; mix at low speed.

4. Pour batter into prepared pan(s) and bake 30 to 40 minutes, until a toothpick inserted into the center of the cake comes out clean and dry. Remove from pan and let cool on a wire rack.

FROM THE KITCHEN OF
CATHERINE WISE

5. Caramel sauce: In a saucepan over low heat, dissolve sugar in water, stirring only once at the beginning before the mixture starts to heat up. Increase heat and bring to a boil; cook until mixture develops a nice caramel color. (If the syrup starts to color unevenly, shake the saucepan back and forth but do not stir.) Add cream and cook about 30 seconds or until cream is thoroughly mixed with syrup. (At this point you may stir with a spoon if necessary.) Remove from heat and immediately transfer to a bowl.

6. To serve: Cut cake into pieces and serve on a plate with fresh peach slices and warm caramel sauce.

Serves 6

SOFT CHOCOLATE CAKE WITH FRESH STRAWBERRIES AND FIGS

PREHEAT OVEN TO 350° F (180° C)
SIX 3/4-CUP (175 mL) CUPCAKE PANS (OR A LARGE MUFFIN TIN),
LIGHTLY BUTTERED AND FLOURED

3/4 cup	unsalted butter	175 mL
6 oz	bittersweet chocolate	175 g
3/4 cup	granulated sugar	175 mL
6 tbsp	all-purpose flour	90 mL
5	large eggs	5
3	figs, halved or quartered	3
3	strawberries, halved or quartered	3
	Icing sugar for garnish	
	Crème Anglaise (optional)	
	Raspberry coulis (optional)	

1. In a double boiler, melt butter and chocolate separately.

2. In a large bowl, mix together sugar and flour, then the eggs. Do not overmix. Add melted chocolate. Gently blend in the melted butter.

3. Pour batter into prepared cupcake pans, three–quarters full. Bake in preheated oven for 5 to 7 minutes.

4. To serve, decorate each plate with crème Anglaise and raspberry coulis, if desired. Arrange the fruit on plates and dust with icing sugar. Turn out the chocolate cupcakes onto the plates and serve warm.

There are a number of organic cane sugars available, ranging in taste from a strong molassesy flavor (Rapunzel) to a mild, mellow one (New Sucanat). Organic sugars yield the same results as white, yellow and brown sugars and can be substituted with equal amounts.

Bittersweet chocolate, a mixture of cocoa butter and sugar, falls between semi-sweetened chocolate and unsweetened chocolate and has a pronounced chocolate flavor.

Variation

Serve with the Ginger Crème Anglaise used in the GINGER-VANILLA BREAD PUDDING recipe (page 174) or the WILD FRUIT DIPPING SAUCE (page 61) and CRÈME FRAÎCHE (page 62).

FROM THE KITCHEN OF
CLAUDE POSTEL

Serves 6 to 8

SOUR CHERRY CLAFOUTI

There are hundreds of varieties of cherries but all of them can be classified as sweet or sour. The most common sweet cherry in North America is the Bing cherry, but sweet cherries come in all colors, shapes and sizes and are best appreciated when eaten raw. Sour cherries, including Montmorency and Morellos, are usually cooked and are often used in liqueurs and canning. Cherries do not continue to ripen once they're picked so avoid fruit that is small, hard and pale. Instead, choose plump, firm cherries that are evenly colored and glossy.

PREHEAT OVEN TO 400° F (200° C)
10-INCH (25 CM) FLAN PAN

3 tbsp	unsalted butter	45 mL
2 tbsp	granulated sugar	25 mL
1 lb	sour cherries, pitted	500 g
1/4 cup	butter	50 mL
2	eggs, beaten	2
2/3 cup	milk	150 mL
1 cup	sugar	250 mL
2/3 cup	all-purpose flour	150 mL
1 1/2 cups	ground almonds	375 mL
Pinch	cinnamon (optional)	Pinch

1. Rub the baking dish with the butter and sprinkle with sugar. (Alternatively, line the flan pan with sweet pastry dough.) Arrange cherries in pan.

2. In a saucepan, melt butter over medium heat and cook until it turns light brown. Remove from heat and allow to cool briefly. Combine the butter with eggs and milk.

4. In a bowl combine sugar, flour, ground almonds and, if using, cinnamon. Stir in milk mixture and mix well. Pour batter over cherries. Bake for 40 to 45 minutes or until set.

Variations

This recipe works well with other fruits, such as raspberries and blueberries (use about 1/2 pint [250 mL]).

FROM THE KITCHEN OF
CHRIS KLUGMAN

**Makes
6 panukas**

PANUKAS
(LATVIAN PANCAKES)

2	eggs, separated	2
3 tbsp	granulated sugar	45 mL
3/4 cup	milk	175 mL
1/2 cup	all-purpose flour	125 mL
1/2 tsp	salt	2 mL
1/2 cup	grated white Cheddar cheese	125 mL
1 cup	berries or chopped apples (acidic fruit is preferable – gooseberries, red or black currants, tart apples, etc.)	250 mL
	Oil for frying	
	Cinnamon and sugar for sprinkling	
	Fresh fruit (optional)	
	Sour cream or CRÈME FRAÎCHE (see recipe, page 62), optional	

1. In a bowl combine yolks and sugar; whisk or beat until light and golden. Add milk and then flour, whisking constantly, until the mixture has the consistency of a thick milkshake. Add salt.

2. When ready to cook, beat egg whites until stiff and fold into batter alternately with cheese and fruit.

3. In a frying pan, heat oil 1/8 to 1/4 inch (2 to 5 mm) deep over medium heat. Scoop about 1/2 cup (125 mL) batter into the pan. (This will spread to 5 to 6 inches [12.5 to 15 cm] in diameter.) Cook slowly enough that the top becomes solid (usually air holes will form). If the heat is too high and the bottom is getting too dark, flip it like a pancake.

4. Sprinkle with cinnamon and sugar. Place on a plate and, if desired, top with more fresh fruit and serve with sour cream or crème fraîche.

There are several varieties of gooseberries found in North America and they range from translucent to opaque, fuzzy to smooth, large to small, sweet to tart and come in all colors. Pick gooseberries that have a rich gloss and are hard and dry. They are often used in jams and jellies (they have a high pectin content) and with meats and poultry. The Cape gooseberry, also known as the ground cherry, is a different fruit from a different family and has a papery husk surrounding the berry.

FROM THE KITCHEN OF
ALLI MILLAR

APPLE BEIGNETS

2	egg yolks	2
3/4 to 1 cup	all-purpose flour	175 to 250 mL
5/8 cup	beer	135 mL
Pinch	salt	Pinch
	A few gratings of nutmeg	
	Oil for frying	
3	egg whites	3
6	firm cooking apples (Northern Spy, Idared, Empire, etc.), peeled, cored and cut into 1/2-inch (1 cm) rings, or cut into eighths	6
	Flour for dredging	
	Sugar or sugar and cinnamon for dusting	

1. Put yolks into a bowl and alternately mix in flour and beer. Add salt and nutmeg. (The mixture should have the consistency of pancake batter; add more flour or beer as required.) Allow to rest, covered, in the refrigerator for 10 minutes.

2. Heat oil in deep fryer to 350° F (180° C). (If not using a deep fryer, use a shallow saucepan; pour oil to depth of about 1/2 inch [1 cm] and heat over medium–high heat.)

3. Whip egg whites and fold gently into batter. Dredge apples in flour; dip into batter. Fry in hot oil for about 30 seconds or until golden brown and crisp. (If the oil is too hot, the beignets will brown too quickly; if it's too cool, they will absorb too much oil. Do not put too many beignets in at once or the oil will cool too much.)

4. Toss beignets in sugar and serve.

While there are some organic all-purpose flours, most organic flours are either hard or soft. If you need to make your own all-purpose flour, mix seven-eighths hard flour to one-eighth soft. Organic flours tend to be less dry than conventional flours, so keep that in mind when you're baking. (A recipe calling for 1 cup [250 mL] of conventional flour, for example, might need 1 cup [250 mL] and 1 tbsp [15 mL] of organic flour, depending on what is being made.)

FROM THE KITCHEN OF
JAMIE KENNEDY

HAINLE VINEYARDS' GINGER-VANILLA BREAD PUDDING LACED WITH LEMON CURD

Serves 4 to 6

PREHEAT OVEN TO 350° F (180° C)

9- BY 5-INCH (2 L) BAKING DISH, GREASED

GINGER CRÈME ANGLAISE

1	2-inch (5 cm) piece ginger root, peeled and sliced	1
4	egg yolks	4
3 tbsp	granulated sugar	45 mL
1 1/2 cups	milk	375 mL
1/2 cup	light (10%) cream	125 mL
1	vanilla bean *or* 1 tsp (5 mL) vanilla extract	1
1 to 2 tbsp	chopped crystallized ginger	15 to 25 mL

LEMON CURD

3	eggs	3
	Juice and zest of 3 lemons	
1/2 cup	granulated sugar	125 mL
1/4 cup	sour cream	50 mL

Half	loaf day-old bread (brioche, challah, French bread, etc.), toasted	Half

1. Ginger crème Anglaise: Place ginger in a saucepan and add just enough water to cover. Bring to a boil; blanch for about 30 seconds. Remove from heat; drain. Set ginger aside.

2. In a bowl combine egg yolks and sugar; whisk until sugar is dissolved.

3. In a saucepan combine milk, cream, vanilla bean and blanched ginger; bring to a boil. Remove from heat and strain mixture through a fine sieve into the egg yolk mixture. Whisk to combine and pour back into saucepan; stir over medium heat until the mixture thickens, about 10 minutes. (The sauce should coat the back of a spoon.)

4. Let cool; add the crystallized ginger.

FROM THE KITCHEN OF
DAVID FORESTELL

5. Lemon curd: In a double boiler, combine eggs, lemon juice, lemon zest, sugar and sour cream. Heat gently, stirring, until thickened, about 15 minutes. Strain through a fine sieve into a bowl.

6. To finish: Moisten bread with ginger crème Anglaise. Layer bread in baking dish with lemon curd. Pour any remaining crème Anglaise over the top. Cover loosely with aluminum foil. Place covered dish into a larger baking dish; add about 1 inch (2.5 cm) hot water to the larger dish. Bake for 20 minutes, remove foil and bake for another 10 to 15 minutes until set.

Serves 6 to 8

CHOCOLATE CUSTARD WITH PLUMS IN WHITE WINE

PREHEAT OVEN TO 350° F (180° C)

6 TO 8 RAMEKIN DISHES OR 1 SHALLOW BAKING DISH

1/2 cup	granulated sugar	125 mL
1/2 cup	sweet white wine	125 mL
4	large plums, sliced	4

CHOCOLATE CUSTARD

1 cup	whipping (35%) cream	250 mL
6 oz	semi-sweet chocolate, chopped into small pieces	175 g
1 cup	2% milk, cold	250 mL
3/4 cup	granulated sugar	175 mL
3	large eggs, beaten	3
1 cup	whipping (35%) cream, whipped	250 mL
	Sugar to taste	
	Mint sprigs	
1	plum, sliced	1

1. In a saucepan bring sugar and wine to a boil; cook 1 to 2 minutes. Stir in the plums. If the plums are not very ripe, cook another 1 to 2 minutes; otherwise, remove from heat. Let cool and strain.

2. Chocolate custard: In a saucepan heat whipping cream just to the boiling point. Put chocolate pieces in a bowl and pour hot cream over. Whisk until chocolate is melted. Stir in milk and sugar. Add eggs; mix thoroughly.

3. Distribute plums equally on bottom of ramekin dishes or baking dish. Pour chocolate custard over plums and fill to 1/4 inch (5 mm) below the top. Bake until custard is set, about 35 to 45 minutes for the ramekins, 45 to 60 minutes for the baking dish, depending on the volume and dimensions of the pan.

4. To finish: Mix whipped cream with sugar to taste. Spoon or pipe whipped cream onto chocolate custard. Garnish with a mint leaf and a piece of fresh plum.

There are more than 2,000 varieties of plums in the world but most consumers are familiar only with a handful of them. California, however, grows about 150 varieties, which accounts for almost 90 percent of the country's plum production. Varieties such as Juneblood, Simka, Yakima, Black Beauty, Casselman and Friar are being distributed across North America – so sample some new ones if you have the opportunity. Look for fully colored fruit that yield slightly to gentle pressure, are not bruised or shriveled and have a fragrant smell.

FROM THE KITCHEN OF
LORENE SAURO

RASPBERRY WHEAT BEER AND APPLE ICE WITH BLOSSOMS

Makes 6 cups (1.5 L)

This ice recipe is very adaptable: any type of apple, fruit-flavored beer and edible flower can be used, depending on desired taste and availability. Different edible flowers, for instance, will provide various flavors: marigolds are slightly musky; nasturtiums are sweet yet peppery; roses are delicately fragrant; lavender flowers are strong and heady; geraniums are citrusy and minty; and violets are sweet. Use organically grown flowers for this recipe or confirm that the flowers have not been treated with chemicals.

CHILL A SHALLOW PAN THAT WILL HOLD 8 CUPS (2 L)

4	assorted apples, peeled and cored	4
1 1/2 cups	raspberry wheat beer or any other fruity beer	375 mL
1 cup	water	250 mL
1 cup	granulated sugar	250 mL
3/4 cup	edible flower petals (see note at left for suggestions)	175 mL
	Mint sprigs	

1. Dice apples into small cubes or roughly chop them in a food processor. Marinate apples in beer for 1 hour.

2. Meanwhile, make the simple syrup: In a saucepan, bring water and sugar to a boil; stir to dissolve all of the sugar.

3. Mix apples, simple syrup and flower petals in the chilled pan. Place in freezer, tossing every 30 minutes, for 3 hours. Serve in delicate cups or hollowed-out apples and garnish with mint sprigs.

FROM THE KITCHEN OF
CHRISTOPH CARL

Serves 6
Makes 4 cups
(1 L)

WILD BLUEBERRY AND MINT ICE CREAM

Wild blueberries are those delectable tiny blueberries found in abundance in the summer. Despite their "wildness," wild blueberries are not considered organic unless they are certified – in some cases the bush may be too close to a farm where pesticides are sprayed, or located along a high-density highway. Former Wabigoon Metis Development Corporation president Lorne Mitchell notes that the OCIA-certified Ontario bush that he managed yielded 30,000 lbs (13,500 kg) of blueberries in one season. Now that's a lot of pies and ice cream!

ICE-CREAM MAKER

1 pint	wild blueberries	500 mL
2 tbsp	kirsch	25 mL
3/4 cup	granulated sugar	175 mL
2 cups	whipping (35%) cream	500 mL
1/2 cup	mint leaves, chopped	125 mL

1. Rinse blueberries, discarding any that are bruised.

2. In a stainless steel saucepan, heat blueberries and kirsch over gentle heat until they are tender and have released their juices. Transfer berries to a blender or food processor; purée. Strain through a sieve to remove the seeds.

3. Measure out 1 cup (250 mL) of the fruit purée. Add sugar and stir until dissolved. Add cream and mint.

4. Chill and freeze in ice-cream maker according to manufacturer's instructions.

FROM THE KITCHEN OF
CLAIRE STUBBS

*Makes 2
dozen cookies*

DOUBLE-CHOCOLATE COOKIES

Good-quality, organically made American and European chocolates are available on the market and are comparable in price to other premium chocolates.

Chocolate bars can be used for home baking, but look for one that has a smooth texture. As well, experiment with different organic chocolates; the sugar used in some can be too strong for certain baked goods and others can change their flavor after being baked.

PREHEAT OVEN TO 350° F (180° C)

4 oz	semi-sweet chocolate, chopped	125 g
1 tbsp	salted butter	15 mL
1	egg	1
1/3 cup	brown sugar	75 mL
1 tbsp	water	15 mL
1 tsp	vanilla extract	5 mL
2 tbsp	all-purpose flour	25 mL
1/2 tsp	baking powder	2 mL
6 oz	semi-sweet chocolate, chopped	175 g
1 cup	walnuts, chopped	250 mL

1. In a double boiler, melt the 4 oz (125 g) of chocolate with the butter. Let cool for about 10 minutes.

2. In a bowl, beat together the egg, brown sugar, water and vanilla. Stir in melted chocolate and butter. Mix flour and baking powder together and add to the chocolate mixture. Fold in the 6 oz (175 g) of chocolate and walnuts.

3. Drop batter by the teaspoonful onto a baking sheet. Bake for 13 to 15 minutes.

FROM THE KITCHEN OF
JOANNE YOLLES

ALMOND CONES FILLED WITH MOUSSE AND FRESH BERRIES

Mascarpone cheese is whipped, sweetened cream cheese and has a luscious, rich and creamy taste. Commonly used in tiramisu, crêpes, tarts and cheesecakes, this smooth unripened cheese can be substituted with an organic cream cheese, which is sometimes available at local farmers' markets.

Kirsch is a clear liqueur made from black cherries that has a very strong flavor and high alcohol content.

PREHEAT OVEN TO 375° F (190° C)
BAKING SHEET, BUTTERED AND FLOURED

ALMOND CONES

3 3/4 cups	sliced almonds	925 mL
1 1/2 cups	granulated sugar	375 mL
1/3 cup	all-purpose flour	75 mL
8	egg whites	8
1/4 cup	melted butter	50 mL

RASPBERRY-MASCARPONE MOUSSE

7	egg yolks	7
	Zest of 1 lemon	
1 cup	granulated sugar	250 mL
1	envelope gelatin (or 4 gelatin leaves)	1
2 tbsp	water	25 mL
1 tbsp	kirsch	15 mL
2 tbsp	whipping (35%) cream	25 mL
1/2 cup	mascarpone cheese	125 mL
1/4 cup	raspberry purée (from about 1/2 cup [125 mL] whole raspberries, processed)	50 mL
4	egg whites, whipped	4
1 1/2 cups	raspberries	375 mL

1. Almond cones: In a bowl combine almonds, sugar and flour; mix well. Add egg whites; mix until batter has a consistent, homogeneous texture. Add butter.

2. Depending on size of baking sheet, pour 8 to 10 tbsp (120 to 150 mL) of batter on sheet, with each cookie 3 inches (7.5 cm) apart; press down with a fork until flat and round. Bake in preheated oven for 10 to 15 minutes or until evenly cooked and golden. Quickly remove them from the baking sheet with a spatula and form into cones by rolling opposite sides of the biscuit together at the middle point of the circle. Allow to cool.

FROM THE KITCHEN OF
ANNE YARYMOWICH &
ROB MACDONALD

3. Mousse: In a stainless steel bowl, combine egg yolks, lemon and sugar; place over a double boiler. Whisk constantly until mixture becomes thick and ribbony and forms a sabayon.

4. In a small pot, soften gelatin in water; melt over low heat. Add kirsch. Add mixture to sabayon and let cool until slightly above room temperature.

5. Mix whipping cream and mascarpone together just until smooth. (Do not to whip too much.) Fold mascarpone mixture and raspberry purée into the sabayon. Fold in the whipped egg whites and raspberries. Refrigerate for 2 hours until mousse is set.

6. To serve: Spoon some of the mousse into almond cones and garnish with berries.

Makes 12
large cookies

SESAME-SPELT FORTUNE COOKIES

This recipe will work with whole or unbleached spelt, oat flour or soft (or pastry) wheat flour, all of which are available organically. Organic or free-range farm eggs yield better results because their whites are stronger than those of commercial eggs.

PREHEAT OVEN TO 350° TO 375° F (180° TO 190° C)

1/2 cup	granulated sugar	125 mL
3	egg whites	3
1/4 tsp	sea salt	1 mL
3/4 cup	spelt flour	175 mL
1 tbsp	sesame seeds	15 mL
1/2 cup	melted butter, cooled slightly	125 mL
1/2 tsp	vanilla extract	2 mL

1. In a bowl stir sugar into egg whites until dissolved. Add sea salt. Whisk in spelt flour followed by the sesame seeds, melted butter and vanilla. Allow to rest for 1 hour.

2. Write your fortune-cookie messages on 1- by 3-inch (2.5 by 7.5 cm) slips of paper and then fold in half. (Two of our favorites are the old Confucian curse, "May you live in interesting times," and "Your turn to help with the dishes.")

3. Scoop batter with a tablespoon and drop on greased cookie sheets (parchment paper won't work here); spread flat with a palette knife. Bake for 6 to 9 minutes until edges turn brown. Edges may start to curl, depending on baking sheet. Cookies will spread to about 4 to 5 inches (10 to 12.5 cm) in diameter.

4. With a spatula or palette knife, loosen cookies from sheets as soon as they are removed from the oven. Place a message on each cookie. Fold cookie in half, then bend or fold again; place in a muffin tin until cooled. (Cookies must be molded while they are still hot, so keep your hands dry and work fast or wear cotton gloves to protect your fingers.)

5. Serve these oversized fortune cookies with small bowls of WILD FRUIT DIPPING SAUCE (see recipe, page 61). After the fortunes have been read, the shards of cookie make excellent spoons.

FROM THE KITCHEN OF
LAUREN BOYINGTON &
CHRIS GUSTAFSSON

Sous chef **Victoria Adams**, who also heads up the bakery kitchen at the River Café on Prince's Island outside of Calgary, believes in sourcing out local, natural products and respecting the rhythms and seasons of the earth. When Adams moved from Toronto to Calgary, she was surprised at the lack of availability and use of organic ingredients so she co-founded Earth to Table, an organization that brings together chefs and organic growers.

The "Aldermeister" at Vancouver's Salmon House on the Hill is chef **Dan Atkinson** and his expertise on the alderwood grill, his love of cooking and his commitment to Pacific Northwest cuisine show on his menu and in his dishes. From his formal training through to his apprenticeships, Atkinson's primary influence has been the West Coast.

Formerly chef at Café La Gaffe, **John Baby**, who is now at Acqua, is an active member of Knives & Forks and its mandate: "The benefits of using organics are many. One is getting to know the people who actually produce our food. Another is the quality of organics. Being locally produced, these foods offer a most amazing array of flavors unavailable from foods engineered to travel in trucks for a week!"

Suzanne Baby travelled extensively for three years throughout Europe and Asia, cooking along the way. She returned to Toronto where she worked at the Windsor Arms Hotel, Bistro 990, Bowers, Splendido and Lakes and then opened a restaurant on Georgian Bay with her husband and brother where they grew much of their own produce organically. Baby is currently chef at the Gallery Grill at University of Toronto's Hart House.

After studying neurophysiology at the University of Toronto, **Lawrence Bangay** decided to switch from medical labs to kitchens and worked at several restaurants before opening his own in Barrie, Ont. Bangay then started Chef's Table Catering and Desserts and is currently focusing his time on his food manufacturing company, Sous Vide Canada.

Karen Barnaby, executive chef of The Fish House in Stanley Park, created her appetizer especially for the Tearoom T in Vancouver, a purveyor, retailer and wholesaler of looseleaf tea. Formerly of David Wood Food Shop in Toronto, Barnaby also teaches cooking classes and has recently had her second cookbook published, *Screamingly Good Food*.

The relationship between the owners of Acton's Grill & Café and its chef, **Werner Bassen**, started in 1975 when they were all at Fenton's in Toronto. Now settled in Wolfville, N.S., Bassen maintains the same philosophy that has earned both restaurants rave reviews: "Freshly prepare as much as you can from scratch, using fresh ingredients — local and organic if possible."

When **Wanda Beaver** graduated from art college she was already baking desserts and selling them to various Toronto restaurants. Twelve years later she has a thriving wholesale business, Wanda's Pie in the Sky, as well as a retail bakery and café. The emphasis at Wanda's is on fresh, handmade baked goods — more than 80 varieties of cakes, cookies, tarts, squares and pies — using only the best ingredients.

Former in-store chef at The St. Clair Market, **Wendy Blackwood** is now the co-ordinator of Loblaws' cooking schools located in Toronto and Bowmanville, Ont. While Blackwood has an extensive background in professional cooking and catering, she also grows flowers, herbs and produce, including specialty and heirloom tomatoes and eight kinds of potatoes.

Starting as a pastry chef and working his way around many kitchens, **Paul Boehmer** has worked at Karin, Scaramouche, Bistro 990, Rhodes, Nekah and Lakes. He has worked with many supporters of the organic movement and while at the Parrot, Boehmer experimented with serving an exclusively organic menu. Currently chef at Opus in Toronto, Boehmer offers a fusion menu with Asian references.

While **Lauren Boyington** was one of the Wild Culture Food Guerillas, she offered close-to-the-hip catering for ecological groups, which included serving multi-course vegetarian meals to 130 campers for five days — on an island without electricity . Her focus continues to be on the use of seasonal, regional and organic and wild foods. Boyington is Knives & Forks' 1998 president and has been the editor of the annual Feast of Fields cookbook since it began publishing in 1991.

Jeff Brandt left the Okanagan Valley for art school in Toronto. While cooking to pay for art supplies, he had the good fortune to work with chefs Claudio Aprile, David Van Den Driesschen, Didier Leroy and Chris MacDonald. Brandt has remained in Toronto and is the chef at Dooney's Café.

As a well-respected butcher and barbecue expert, **David Brown,** president of Meat Consultants International Inc., advises on setting standards for meat in Canada and also trains federal government meat inspectors. Brown had the honor of staging a barbecue for Julia Child and 200 of her friends, created Toronto's Foodshare Barbecue to feed the hungry and homeless, and on average, barbecues for more than 20,000 people each summer.

After catering in London for a few years, Scotsman **Robert Buchanan** moved to Canada where he has worked at the Windsor Arms Hotel, Scaramouche, Bowers and the Millcroft Inn. For the past four years he has been the chef at Toronto's Acqua, and for the past two he has also been a co-owner.

With a fashion degree in hand, P.E.I. native **Melva Buell** travelled to Europe where she found herself working in an Amsterdam hotel kitchen and she's never looked back. She went on to study at the Culinary Institute of America, owned her own restaurants and catering companies in Atlantic Canada and is now catering and consulting in Toronto. Buell has always been a supporter of organically grown products, both at home and in her professional kitchens.

Christoph Carl honed his art of cooking in kitchens in Ottawa, Kitchener, Toronto and Whistler before settling down at his family's Old Country House Restaurant in Haliburton, Ont. While studying across Canada, Carl developed a unique fresh style that is ever-present in his menus and is committed to buying his ingredients from local and organic farms and markets.

Anthony Carrozza, chef and co-owner of Villaggio's Restaurant in Toronto has been delighting diners with his menus for more than 20 years. Meticulous attention to visual detail in addition to the combination of elegant atmosphere and carefully prepared dishes reveal a strong influence from his mentor, Arpie Magar.

While working in Italy, **David Catenaro**, chef di cucina of Ciao Bella Restaurant, became passionate about risotto, so he shares this love with daily specials at the restaurant. Catenaro feels that freshness and simplicity enhances the foods' natural flavor and he supports and showcases Ontario farmers' products throughout the growing season.

Brad Clease has been cooking for 11 years and says "it's like another sense. I love it. I always knew what I wanted to do. Good food and wine is a necessity." Clease's enthusiasm is currently being spread around Vancouver, where he is the chef at Raintree on the Landing.

By combining the cultural influences and culinary experiences he encountered while travelling around the world, **Frederic Couton** has brought a new cooking style to the Cannery Seafood House in Vancouver. Couton says that he prefers to make the most of seasonal, local produce — almost three-quarters of his ingredients are B.C. products — because he can cook them simply and let their fresh flavors take over the plate.

French-born **Dominique Crevoisier** worked in several top restaurants in France, Switzerland, England and Germany before emigrating to Canada in 1975. Before joining Montreal's Restaurant Les Halles in 1980, he worked in other fine establishments in Montreal, Quebec and Edmonton. Although Crevoisier has had 30 years of international culinary experience, he says he still loves his work and is constantly trying to improve.

Andrea Damon Gibson is baker and owner of Fred's Breads, a purveyor of high quality sourdough breads made with natural ingredients and organic flours. All of Fred's Breads are developed with a natural yeast starter, hand-shaped, hearth-baked and ripened at a low temperature, which results in an intense flavor, crisp crust and a slightly chewy crumb. Before opening her own Toronto bakery, Damon Gibson was pastry chef at Splendido for several years.

Executive chef **Bryan Davidson** works at Kingdom Café at Vegetable Kingdom, which sells exclusively organic foods, as well as Oasis in Toronto. He has catered and taught Aboriginal cuisine, worked at Fenton's, Elmwood Dining Club, Byzantium and Carlevale's, and believes that "the best possible ingredients are organic."

As a Kent State graduate of surface design, **Pandora de Green** first became a pasta-maker in Massachusetts and then moved to Canada where she worked in several Stratford restaurants before opening her own business, Pan Chancho Bakery in Kingston. After selling her bakery, de Green returned to the States and is currently the pastry chef at the Flying Fish Restaurant in Seattle, Wash.

Hillebrand's Vineyard Café chef de cuisine, **Antonio de Luca**, was captivated by the art of food preparation from an early age because his family had a restaurant in Italy. Since he joined the culinary profession, he has worked in England, Germany and at several Ontario restaurants. De Luca prefers a rural setting, such as the vineyard in Niagara-on-the-Lake, which is surrounded by farms – ideal for a chef who wants the freshest ingredients possible.

Tim D'Souza is a graduate of the Italian culinary program at Toronto's George Brown College. While in Italy, he worked there and in England before returning to Toronto where he is the restaurant chef at Accents in the Sutton Place Hotel.

The Four Seasons Hotel, King Edward Hotel, Pronto, Scaramouche, Bistro 990 and Canoe have all been home to **Jeff Dueck**, who is now chef-partner at Live! At the Mississauga restaurant, Dueck emphasizes the use of fresh ingredients and features Canadian foods, such as seafood from the Maritimes and beef from Alberta.

After working in Toronto at numerous restaurants including Le Rendezvous, Oliver's Bistro, Scaramouche and Bowers, **David Eaglesham** decided to hang his chef toque up and learn the art of cheesemaking at a goat farm in Indiana. He plans to travel around the States for a year or so discovering all he can about dairy production and then will possibly become a cheesemaker himself.

Born in Mendoza, Argentina, **Elena Embrioni's** interest in cooking was nurtured at an early age by her grandmother, who inspired feeding frenzies in her large family. Embrioni found her destiny through "cooking from the heart" and has been serving legions of fans at Toronto's Southern Accent Restaurant for several years. She shares some of her culinary secrets in *The Southern Accent Cajun and Creole Cookbook*, which she co-wrote with co-owner Frances Wood.

Inspired by traditional Canadian foods sprinkled with Native influences, chef **Dwayne Ennest** has developed "wood-fired cuisine of the Northwest" – such as smoked arctic char, spruce balsa jelly, air-dried buffalo and bannock – for the River Café in Calgary. Formerly of Teatro and Mescalero, Ennest leans toward healthy, organic foods and he strongly believes in travelling as much as possible to explore a world of new food ideas.

As a natural-foods store owner, baker, one of the owner-chefs of Ottawa's Green Door Restaurant (which serves almost exclusively organic food), and gardener of two acres of vegetables, **Ron Farmer** has come to value local, seasonal and organically grown food "for its taste and nutritional benefits, its environmental sustainability and as a livelihood."

Raised and schooled in Toronto, chef **David Feys** travelled west to join the creative kitchens of Vancouver Island's noted Sooke Harbour House. Today, as principal of Feys & Hobbs, a Victoria-based catering and events enterprise, Feys draws Canadian, American and overseas clients seeking his unique West Coast cuisine and "sense of occasion."

"Mother Nature knows best," says **Renée Foote**, who likes to work with locally grown organic produce because of its incomparable flavor and freshness. The Mercer St. Grill co-owner and chef has an eclectic background that matches her cooking style: chef at Byzantium, lunch chef at Messis, pastry chef at North 44° and lunch saucier at Sutton Place Hotel.

Albertan **David Forestell**, chef at Hainle Vineyards' Amphora Bistro in Peachland, B.C., began his culinary career in Los Angeles, working at Campanile, La Brea and Patina. He returned to Alberta and worked at the Buffalo Mountain Lodge in Banff, where he developed Rocky Mountain cuisine, then moved on to the River Café, Savoir Faire and Options in Calgary.

British-born **Keith Froggett** came to Canada in 1979 and has worked at the Four Seasons, Sutton Place Hotel and Fenton's. Since 1983 he has been chef at Scaramouche where he has won many accolades for his innovative cuisine and exquisite presentations; he has since become a co-owner. Froggett doesn't let all the attention faze him, "I like to stay away from all the glitz and just serve good food."

Daniel Gilbert opened Daniel's of Nobleton in 1980 and quickly established a reputation for fine, creative cuisine that features local, seasonal and organic food. Because fresh ingredients are the backbone of his cooking philosophy and to accommodate the rapidly changing seasons, Gilbert creates a new menu each month. As a board member of Knives & Forks and the chair of the past few Feast of Fields, Gilbert is a strong advocate of organic agriculture.

Chris Gustafsson enjoys cooking for folks and has helped different field kitchens from Food Not Bombs and Seeds of Peace to nourishing activists working to preserve old-growth forests. When everything else goes wrong, Gustafsson believes that food will always be healing. He sees organic food as the cleanest way to support our value-added green economy.

The philosophy of Feastabilities Inc., a catering company run by **Jonathan Hill** and Stephanie Hill, embraces diversity, creativity and excellent ingredients. The pair has a passion for all culinary experiences and likes to make traditional dishes with a twist; they do this at The Advocates' Society dining room in the Sir William Campbell House in Toronto.

As co-owner of Herbs Fine Foods & Catering and sous-chef at Herbs Restaurant, **Mark Howatt** has his plate full. And that's who his retail store is marketed to – busy professionals. Specializing in prepared dinners, breads, desserts and pastries, the gourmet shop is an extension of the restaurant's philosophy: fresh, homemade market foods using organic and seasonal ingredients.

Gary Hoyer is a long-time supporter of organic foods and is a former board member of Knives & Forks. He keeps busy with Millie's Bistro & Gourmet Market, a manufacturing company, catering and teaching. His recipes in this cookbook are designed as tasting dishes and he suggests that readers "use the components individually or in conjunction with other components. Have fun and enjoy!"

Matthew Jamieson grew up in Stamford, Conn., studied at La Varenne in Paris and apprenticed in Boston. After opening the popular Mad Apples in Toronto, he sold the business to open another restaurant, Sierra Grill in Barrie, Ont. Since then Jamieson has been cooking, catering and teaching and he recently opened the Woodside Restaurant in Orangeville, Ont. to full houses. Jamieson is a former Knives & Forks board member.

Bill Jones is a European-trained chef whose work experience includes top restaurants in Canada, England and France. Magnetic North Cuisine, his consulting company, is a strong supporter of the local food industry and active in the promotion of regional products and cuisine. Jones is a charter member of Cuisine Canada, was a key organizer of Northern Bounty II in Vancouver, is a past-chair of FarmFolk/CityFolk and had been an active participant in all of the Feast of Fields to date.

With a degree in languages, **Izabela Kalabis** went to Europe where she decided to enroll in the cooking school La Varenne. After training and working in several fine restaurants in France, she returned to Canada to become chef at Inniskillin Wines as well as a private caterer. In both kitchens, Kalabis believes that "organic foods imply a certain lifestyle, including sound nutritional values and superior taste. The desire to use better ingredients should be everyone's goal."

While Ethiopian **Assefa Kebede** has cooked and travelled in many parts of Africa to learn about its different cuisines, it was only a hobby at first, admits the U.B.C. agricultural science graduate. His Vancouver restaurant, Nyala African Cuisine, has participated in Feast of Fields and the Vancouver Folk Music Festival, where he was proud to introduce Ethiopian food to many new palates.

"Cooking with products that are indigenous to an area puts people at ease for intangible reasons," says **Jamie Kennedy** of J.K. ROM. Kennedy's emphasis on locally grown organic ingredients has been influential in defining Canadian cuisine. As a co-founder of Knives & Forks, Kennedy has been instrumental in promoting organic agriculture within the restaurant community and among consumers and has helped nurture relationships between chefs and farmers.

Jeremy King is the chef and catering team leader at Alternatives' cooking studio in Oakville, Ont. and has worked in the food industry since he was 14, taking time off to study at George Brown College. His skills come "naturally" to him having grown up on an organic hobby farm and having enjoyed organic foods most of his life. King is actively involved in Knives & Forks and in the promotion of organic food and agriculture.

As executive chef at the Rosewater Supper Club, **Chris Klugman** has brought his philosophy of purity, freshness and enlightened cuisine to discriminating Toronto diners. "It's not enough for food to be just tasty and it's not enough for food to be just healthy. It must be both to be good food," he believes. Klugman is a charter member of Knives & Forks, menu consultant, low-fat caterer and a popular guest on television cooking shows.

The four-star Auberge Hatley in North Hatley, Que. has been **Alain Labrie**'s home since 1989. And why not? With the inn's million-dollar greenhouse, Labrie has the liberty that few chefs in Canada have — year-round organic herbs, salad greens and edible flowers at his kitchen doorstep. Labrie worked in a couple hotels before joining Auberge Hatley as chef de cuisine and he has continued his culinary training with stints in French hotels.

With more than 18 years in the restaurant industry, award-winning **Normand Laprise** has made a strong impression around the world as the co-owner and executive chef of the highly acclaimed Restaurant Toqué! in Montreal. In the role of consulting executive chef, Laprise recently opened CENA Restaurant in New York City and has been a guest chef in Tokyo, Bermuda, Toronto and several New York City restaurants.

Brad Long, executive chef at 360, the restaurant atop the CN Tower, explains his cooking philosophy: "I find passion in things some people might take for granted. Textures. Flavors. Colors. I like combining them in new, exciting ways." With a mandate to produce fresh market cuisine using Canadian ingredients whenever possible, Long blends the familiar with the unfamiliar to create spectacular dishes that match the view.

Working tours in California, Hawaii and New York have given **Rob MacDonald** more insight on how other kitchens run — and he's worked in some of the finest in P.E.I., Quebec and Ontario including Maplelawn Café, Mildred Pierce, Scaramouche and Palmerston. MacDonald was one of the chefs to launch the first Feast of Fields in Toronto; he also donates time to prepare dinners for the homeless and less fortunate in Ottawa, where he works at Bella's Bistro.

Growing up in Central Ontario, **Jackie MacKay** found herself working in the restaurant industry when she was 15 and decided to pursue the field at George Brown College. She spent two years travelling and working throughout France and then returned to Toronto to become executive chef at the Wellington Bistro and Mayfair Lakeshore Club. For several years MacKay has been chef de maison for a private home.

After selling his two restaurants, Living Well and Whitlocks, **Dino Magnatta** began travelling again as he believes that world travel helps develop his cooking and winemaking skills. Magnatta learned his craft in France and soon became as passionate about wine as he was about food; several of "Dino's vinos" have received medals at the Intervin International Wine Competition.

Seafood specialist **Michael Mandato** graduated from the Culinary Institute of America and began working in a series of well known Manhattan restaurants including Lafayette, La Côte Basque and Tavern on the Green. Since he's moved northward to Toronto, Mandato has been executive chef at the Senator and is currently sous chef at Chiaro's at the Royal Meriden King Edward Hotel.

Since 1976 **Mark McEwan** has been on the Toronto culinary scene where he's worked at Sutton Place Hotel and Pronto, dazzling diners with his internationally inspired presentations of fresh ingredients. After he opened his North 44° in 1990, he's earned more recognition for his creative mix of Californian, Asian and Italian food and his extensive wine list. His second restaurant, Terra Restaurant Oyster & Martini Bar, opened in 1995.

Glenn McIvor is the owner of Vancouver's Spumante's Café, a Northern Italian restaurant in the heart of Little Italy. As a participant of Feast of Fields, McIvor says "it's great to get together to meet and see what other people are doing in the industry, and to meet the organic growers and suppliers."

Steven McKinley moved from Toronto to Vancouver where he easily adopted a Pacific Northwest style of cooking. As chef at Kilby's Restaurant, a small village bistro in North Vancouver, McKinley has the opportunity to feature local, seasonal food, which he finds in abundance.

With 25 years' culinary experience, **Allison Millar** has owned and operated five restaurants in Toronto, developed a catering business and three restaurants in Latvia, and worked in London, New York City and Stratford, Ont. Alli's Catering provides services in the Toronto area and sells fresh baked goods at the St. Lawrence Farmers' Market, north side, every Saturday. Millar has participated in every Feast of Fields to date.

Andrew Milne-Allan put himself through art school in New Zealand by cooking and "the cooking got out of hand." Since the world traveller has been in Toronto he's owned a few restaurants including Trattoria Giancarlo and the Parrot and worked in many others. He opened Zucca in 1996 with partner Luis Alves, which features contemporary regional Italian cuisine with an emphasis on fresh herbs, vegetables, fish and seafood.

Mark Mogensen has enjoyed his career at such fine Toronto restaurants as Winston's and Bistro 990, as well as the renowned kitchens of King Ranch Health Spa & Fitness Resort and Manitouwaning Lodge. With his former post at HealthWinds and his current one at Husky Injection, he has been even more committed to the art of easy-to-prepare, low-fat, healthful cuisine made extraordinary with fresh ingredients, creative presentation and delectable flavor.

Formerly the chef at Samfira Restaurant in Hamilton, Ont. and currently the manager of the McMaster University Faculty Club, **Mark Mougenot** continues to strive to use local, organically produced foods. Mougenot feels that good food relies on the quality and integrity of the raw ingredients used.

Originally from Moncton, **Dale Nichols** made a sojourn to Toronto where he worked at the Sutton Place Hotel, Pronto, Acrobat Restaurant, Wellington Bistro, North 44° and Canoe before returning to the East Coast as Hotel Halifax's executive chef. Nichols draws heavily on the bounty of local products from the land and the sea, and he recently took home top honors at a Nova Scotia Association of Chefs and Cooks competition.

Toronto chef and owner **Anthony Nuth** opened Herbs Restaurant in 1992 and with a partner, Herbs Fine Foods & Catering in 1997. The Ottawa native's culinary education began in Europe where he worked in several multi-starred restaurants. This period influenced his cooking style, which focuses on modern French cuisine using fresh, seasonal market produce.

Adrienne O'Callaghan trained at Ballymaloe Cookery School in County Cork, Ireland and then went on to work at Drimcong House in County Galway and London's Park Lane Hotel. As the chef at Vancouver's bistro-style restaurant Irish Heather, she is busy interpreting contemporary Irish food in the context of West Coast Canada.

As chef-owner of Mad Apples in Toronto, **Peter Ochitwa** has charmed critics and customers with the neighborhood bistro's innovative cuisine and award-winning wine selection. Ochitwa considers himself an eternal apprentice and is constantly honing his skills; he is involved with several industry committees and organizations.

After working in Paris and opening his first restaurant in London, **Charles Part** came to Canada where he's opened restaurants in Ontario and Quebec. With his wife, Jennifer, Part runs Restaurant Les Fougères in Chelsea, Que. where they are continuing their support of organic food; they have participated in two Feast of Fields, one in Toronto and the other in Ottawa. Part gets his inspiration from organic ingredients and concentrates on their flavors, tastes and textures.

Daina Paulius, who owned the Toronto catering company Daina's In the Kitchen Too, has recently moved to British Columbia to follow her spiritual path.

Honored by the Toronto Escoffier Society as Chef of the Year in 1996, **Kenneth Peace**, chef de cuisine at the Hummingbird Centre for the Performing Arts, believes that a chef never ceases to learn. A respected businessman, educator, mentor, volunteer and charter member of Knives & Forks, Peace works closely with local farmers and emphasizes organic products.

Mark Picone and his kitchen brigade share Vineland Estates Winery's mandate to encourage, promote and capitalize on Niagara's bounty. The spectacular St. Urban Vineyard that surrounds the winery was the site of the 1990 Feast of Fields.

At the young age of 17, **Claude Postel** began his career in Paris and after only a couple years in the business he won awards and praise from *Gault et Millau Guide* and *Michelin Guide* and was recognized as France's youngest chef. In 1983 Postel crossed the Atlantic Ocean and moved to Montreal, where he has established several restaurants and pâtisseries that bear his name.

Organic shiitake grower **Bruno Pretto** of Fun Guy Farms was born in Verona, Italy and came to Canada where he's done everything from earning a chemistry degree and studying cooking to designing and distributing leather goods and helping to manufacture natural juices. Pretto is the only certified mushroom farmer in Ontario and also sells cultivation kits and other mycological supplies.

Extensive travel and his post as executive chef at Toronto's World Trade Centre has allowed **Herbert Pryke** a hands-on opportunity to study the culinary secrets of many unique countries. Currently at the Tasting Rooms, his experiences in Europe, Asia and the Caribbean are reflected in the dishes he prepares, which incorporates many international influences.

Michael Sabo has been cooking in Toronto for more than a decade and has been chef de cuisine at the Estates of Sunnybrook for about half that period. Sabo has been around farms and organic food for most of his life and draws inspiration from his Hungarian roots, developing old family recipes with a modern twist. When using the best quality, raw ingredients, Sabo believes simplicity is the best recipe for success.

As executive chef, **James Saunders** was instrumental in the recent opening of the Waterside Inn in Port Credit, Ont., where he also manages Breakwater Restaurant and the inn's banquet facilities. The British-born chef has worked in many restaurants in Europe and also at the Sherwood Inn in Ontario's Muskoka region. While there, he often foraged around the woods for wild mushrooms and would let "the colors and flavors do all the talking."

Pastry chef **Lorene Sauro** has built a strong following of discerning dessert lovers through her businesses Beyond Words Dessert and Nature's Song Organic Bakery. A past-president of Knives & Forks, Sauro spends a lot of time promoting the virtues of organics: "Quality in food only comes from a sincere commitment to achieve it. Organically grown food, at its best, is the ultimate reflection of sincere commitment and therefore, the ultimate in food quality."

With a masters degree from Columbia University in nutritional and medical anthropology, **Lisa Slater** has moved from both the field and the region. While she has worked in the business for dozens of years, one of Slater's greatest accomplishments has been opening 12 BakeWorks locations in southern Ontario. Her baking philosophy is "keep it simple, keep it good."

Steve Song left a career in investment banking for pastries and desserts. After studying at the Peter Kump School of Culinary Arts in New York, Song worked at Mesa Grill and Restaurant Daniel in New York and the Left Bank and Canoe in Toronto.

Eigensinn Farm in Singhampton, Ont. is where **Michael Stadtländer** has settled down to run his not-so-quiet "restaurant" with his family. The co-founder of Knives & Forks has always appreciated the connection between the chef and the farmer and the rhythms of organic agriculture. At Eigensinn Farm, Stadtländer experiences it all firsthand with the celebration of the cycles of gardening, harvesting, foraging, cooking and eating.

As a graduate of Stratford Chefs School and former apprentice at Sooke Harbour House, **Claire Stubbs**, who is now chef at Mildred Pierce Restaurant, has adopted the philosophy of creating menus around the availability of fresh, locally grown, seasonal products. Mildred Pierce encourages new relationships with local growers and understands the importance and economic sense of supporting local farms and buying produce with superior flavor and freshness.

A vital pulse in the Toronto restaurant scene for more than a dozen years, **Lili Sullivan**, former Auberge du Pommier sous chef and Chapeau chef, is a strong supporter of organic farming and regional and seasonal cuisine. Sullivan is currently chef at The Rebel House and also a consultant specializing in menu and recipe development, a board member of Knives & Forks and an executive member of the Women's Culinary Network.

Armed with chef's papers, an accountancy degree and a programmer analyst diploma, Belgian **Walter Telemans** pursued all three fields until he decided to follow his creativity. He has helped open several restaurants in Calgary, Vancouver and Victoria and is now executive chef at Options in Calgary. Telemans believes that "organic cooking is the future — the best natural ingredients are unmodified and chemical-free. With Options, we are pushing this concept to extremes."

For the past eight years **Frank Von Zuben** has been the breakfast and lunch chef at the legendary Sooke Harbour House, which is surrounded by intoxicating gardens of organically grown edible flowers, herbs and vegetables. Working with freshly caught or harvested seafood (such as gooseneck barnacles and limpets) and the abundance of produce just steps away gives Von Zuben "a sense of goodness while working with the dish." The flavor is the dish."

Becky Waldner of the Wolmsley Elm in Winnipeg shares her philosophy on cooking with organically grown food: "I think it is very important to go back to a more natural way of cooking. The food is more healthy and tasty and you get healthier people as a result."

David Watt attended catering college in England where he apprenticed at London's Ritz Hotel and worked as one of King Hussein's personal chefs. When he returned to Toronto he worked at the Sutton Place Hotel and then moved to Unionville to work at the Pineapple Inn and Blacksmith's Bistro, where he shucked close to 30,000 oysters in one year. Watt now runs his own company, David Watt Catering.

A graduate of the culinary management program at George Brown College, **Stewart Webb** has worked at Le Bistingo, Scaramouche, Bowers and Azalea. As the owner of By David's Catering in Toronto he is now a caterer to the stars, serving at film locations and sets in southern Ontario.

Catherine Wise received her professional training at Leith's School of Food and Wine in London, the Culinary Center of New York and the International Pastry Arts Center with a White House master pastry chef. Now in Ottawa running Black Cat Catering and Consulting, Wise continues her commitment to use organic products and raise the awareness of her clients to the quality and superiority of organically grown food.

Recently chef at Green Gates in Headingley, Man., **Jason Wortzman** has worked and trained in Winnipeg, Montreal, the Laurentians, France, London and Delhi, where he opened an Italian restaurant. At Green Gates Wortzman focused on regional cuisine using local game such as rabbit, pheasant, wild boar and caribou and organic vegetables. Using the same philosophy, Wortzman is planning to manufacture fine food products for the gourmet market.

It is somehow fitting that **Anne Yarymowich** is chef of Agora Restaurant at the Art Gallery of Ontario, as she has a degree in fine arts and photography. Yarymowich has worked at Le Select Bistro and the Parrot, and before taking the helm at Agora, she was chef at Mildred Pierce. Dedicated to the promotion of organic and local products, she combines urban ethnic styles with seasonal ingredients to create Canadian contemporary cuisine.

These days **Joanne Yolles** is more likely to be whipping up a batch of cookies for her two children than a decadent dessert. After working with Jamie Kennedy and Michael Stadtländer at Scaramouche, Yolles went on to Tante Marie's Cooking School in San Francisco and then later returned to Scaramouche where she was pastry chef for many years. Yolles left the restaurant to become an at-home mother but she periodically teaches pastry classes with Great Cooks.